TERRORISM

Opposing Viewpoints®

TERRORISM

Opposing Viewpoints®

Other Books of Related Interest

TERRORISM

Opposing Viewpoints®

Laura K. Egendorf, *Book Editor*

Bonnie Szumski, *Publisher*
Scott Barbour, *Managing Editor*
Helen Cothran, *Senior Editor*

OPPOSING
VIEWPOINTS®
SERIES

GREENHAVEN
PRESS®

THOMSON
———✴———™
GALE

San Diego • Detroit • New York • San Francisco • Cleveland
New Haven, Conn. • Waterville, Maine • London • Munich

LIBRARY OF CONGRESS CATALOGING-IN-PUBLICATION DATA

Terrorism / Laura K. Egendorf, book editor.
    p. cm. — (Opposing viewpoints series)
    Includes bibliographical references and index.
    ISBN 0-7377-2247-9 (pbk. : alk. paper) — ISBN 0-7377-2246-0 (lib. : alk. paper)
      1. Terrorism. 2. Terrorism—United States. 3. National security—United States.
    4. War on Terrorism, 2001– . I. Egendorf, Laura K., 1973– . II. Opposing
    viewpoints series (Unnumbered)
    HV6431.T444 2004
    303.6'25—dc22
                                                                      2003049497

> "Congress shall make no law...abridging the freedom of speech, or of the press."

First Amendment to the U.S. Constitution

The basic foundation of our democracy is the First Amendment guarantee of freedom of expression. The Opposing Viewpoints Series is dedicated to the concept of this basic freedom and the idea that it is more important to practice it than to enshrine it.

Contents

Why Consider Opposing Viewpoints?

"The only way in which a human being can make some approach to knowing the whole of a subject is by hearing what can be said about it by persons of every variety of opinion and studying all modes in which it can be looked at by every character of mind. No wise man ever acquired his wisdom in any mode but this."

John Stuart Mill

In our media-intensive culture it is not difficult to find differing opinions. Thousands of newspapers and magazines and dozens of radio and television talk shows resound with differing points of view. The difficulty lies in deciding which opinion to agree with and which "experts" seem the most credible. The more inundated we become with differing opinions and claims, the more essential it is to hone critical reading and thinking skills to evaluate these ideas. Opposing Viewpoints books address this problem directly by presenting stimulating debates that can be used to enhance and teach these skills. The varied opinions contained in each book examine many different aspects of a single issue. While examining these conveniently edited opposing views, readers can develop critical thinking skills such as the ability to compare and contrast authors' credibility, facts, argumentation styles, use of persuasive techniques, and other stylistic tools. In short, the Opposing Viewpoints Series is an ideal way to attain the higher-level thinking and reading skills so essential in a culture of diverse and contradictory opinions.

In addition to providing a tool for critical thinking, Opposing Viewpoints books challenge readers to question their own strongly held opinions and assumptions. Most people form their opinions on the basis of upbringing, peer pressure, and personal, cultural, or professional bias. By reading carefully balanced opposing views, readers must directly confront new ideas as well as the opinions of those with whom they disagree. This is not to simplistically argue that everyone who reads opposing views will—or should—change his or her opinion. Instead, the series enhances readers' understanding of their own views by encouraging confrontation with opposing ideas. Careful examination of others' views can lead to the readers' understanding of the logical inconsistencies in their own opinions, perspective on why they hold an opinion, and the consideration of the possibility that their opinion requires further evaluation.

Evaluating Other Opinions

To ensure that this type of examination occurs, Opposing Viewpoints books present all types of opinions. Prominent spokespeople on different sides of each issue as well as well-known professionals from many disciplines challenge the reader. An additional goal of the series is to provide a forum for other, less known, or even unpopular viewpoints. The opinion of an ordinary person who has had to make the decision to cut off life support from a terminally ill relative, for example, may be just as valuable and provide just as much insight as a medical ethicist's professional opinion. The editors have two additional purposes in including these less known views. One, the editors encourage readers to respect others' opinions—even when not enhanced by professional credibility. It is only by reading or listening to and objectively evaluating others' ideas that one can determine whether they are worthy of consideration. Two, the inclusion of such viewpoints encourages the important critical thinking skill of objectively evaluating an author's credentials and bias. This evaluation will illuminate an author's reasons for taking a particular stance on an issue and will aid in readers' evaluation of the author's ideas.

It is our hope that these books will give readers a deeper understanding of the issues debated and an appreciation of the complexity of even seemingly simple issues when good and honest people disagree. This awareness is particularly important in a democratic society such as ours in which people enter into public debate to determine the common good. Those with whom one disagrees should not be regarded as enemies but rather as people whose views deserve careful examination and may shed light on one's own.

Thomas Jefferson once said that "difference of opinion leads to inquiry, and inquiry to truth." Jefferson, a broadly educated man, argued that "if a nation expects to be ignorant and free . . . it expects what never was and never will be." As individuals and as a nation, it is imperative that we consider the opinions of others and examine them with skill and discernment. The Opposing Viewpoints Series is intended to help readers achieve this goal.

David L. Bender and Bruno Leone,
Founders

Greenhaven Press anthologies primarily consist of previously published material taken from a variety of sources, including periodicals, books, scholarly journals, newspapers, government documents, and position papers from private and public organizations. These original sources are often edited for length and to ensure their accessibility for a young adult audience. The anthology editors also change the original titles of these works in order to clearly present the main thesis of each viewpoint and to explicitly indicate the opinion presented in the viewpoint. These alterations are made in consideration of both the reading and comprehension levels of a young adult audience. Every effort is made to ensure that Greenhaven Press accurately reflects the original intent of the authors included in this anthology.

Introduction

"A [new] intelligence structure is urgently needed if we are going to avoid another tragedy like September 11."
Bill Gertz, *author of* Breakdown: How America's Intelligence Failures Led to September 11

On September 11, 2001, American history was forever changed when nineteen Middle Eastern hijackers commandeered four commercial airplanes. Two of the planes were flown directly into New York City's World Trade Center, causing the Twin Towers to collapse and creating massive casualties; a third plane was flown into the Pentagon, leading to significant structural damage and additional injuries and fatalities; the final jet crashed into a Pennsylvania field following a struggle between the passengers and hijackers. All told, more than three thousand people died in a seemingly unimaginable act of terrorism. The attacks were soon linked to terrorist plotter Osama bin Laden and the al-Qaeda terrorist network.

At first the events of September 11 seemed to be something that no one could have predicted; not once in the previous history of hijacking had assailants flown planes into buildings. Gradually, however, Americans learned that U.S. intelligence agencies had known prior to September 2001 that such a terrorist attack was possible; unfortunately, the FBI's and CIA's information was incomplete, and neither agency took action that might have helped prevent the tragedy. The discovery that the attacks might have been prevented sparked widespread discussion as to why America's intelligence agencies failed so tragically.

The first problem faced by intelligence agencies was their inability to gather critical information on known terrorists. In December 2002 the Senate Select Committee on Intelligence and the House Permanent Select Committee on Intelligence issued the results of a joint inquiry into the events of September 11. In their report the committees concluded that the intelligence community knew by the summer of 2001 that bin Laden and al-Qaeda were plotting an imminent attack "against U.S. interests." However, the committees asserted, "Prior to September 11, 2001, the Intelligence Community did not effectively develop and use human sources to penetrate the al-Qa'ida inner circle. This lack of reliable and knowledgeable human sources significantly limited the Community's ability to acquire intelligence that could be acted upon before the September 11 attacks."

Of the factors that have been identified to explain the failure of American intelligence agencies to successfully infiltrate al-Qaeda, one that has received particular attention is the lack of agents who could speak or write Arabic. Prior to September 2001, only twenty-one FBI agents knew Arabic, according to the congressional report. The consequences of this limited knowledge of Arabic are serious, as former CIA inspector general Frederick A. Hitz explains. He writes, "As difficult as it may be to recruit an informant in a terrorist cell of individuals willing to expend their lives in suicide missions, it's impossible if you don't speak or read the language and understand the culture from which they come."

A greater problem, however, is that not only did the CIA and FBI lack the ability to infiltrate terrorist cells, but when agents uncovered information about potential terrorists, their findings were often ignored. In two separate cases that occurred during the summer of 2001, FBI agents learned about men who were suspected of being Islamic terrorists enrolling in flight schools. When Bill Kurtz, a supervisor at the FBI's Phoenix office, and his team of agents—in particular counterterrorism agent Kenneth Williams—made such a discovery in July 2001, they sent a memo to FBI headquarters urging the monitoring of flight schools throughout the country. The memo was ignored. In August 2001 the FBI office in Minneapolis found that Zacarias Moussaoui, a foreign-born student at the Pan Am Flight Academy in Eagan, Minnesota, was learning to fly a Boeing 747. The employee from the flight academy who contacted the FBI was particularly concerned because Moussaoui was interested only in flying the plane once it was in the air, not in learning how to take off or land. Suspecting that Moussaoui was a potential hijacker, FBI investigators attempted to get a warrant to search his computer but were refused because there was no "probable cause" that the man had committed a crime. Moussaoui was later discovered to have ties to al-Qaeda and the September 11 plot.

Another reason why key intelligence information was not always acted upon was "the Wall," the name given to guidelines issued in 1995 that governed contacts between FBI agents working on different terrorism cases. As explained by Heather MacDonald, a contributing editor to *City Journal*, the Wall made it nearly impossible for agents to share information that could have strengthened each others' investigations because any exchange of information first had to be approved by FBI headquarters. The problem, as MacDonald explains, is that the Washington office would not "have the ground-level knowledge necessary to understand the potential significance to each investigator of [the information]."

In light of these intelligence failures, intelligence agencies have developed more effective ways to discover and prevent future acts of terrorism. The FBI has nearly doubled the number of counterterrorism agents since September 2001, from thirteen hundred to twenty-five hundred, and hired more than one hundred Arabic-speaking linguists. The CIA has also hired more agents and has had its budget increased by several billion dollars. The FBI and CIA have also coordinated their efforts through daily meetings between their directors and have created the Terrorist Threat Integration Center, a partnership between the FBI, CIA, Department of Homeland Security, and other related agencies that will improve communication within the intelligence community.

The attacks of September 11, 2001, proved that not even the world's lone superpower can protect itself against all enemies. However, changes in the FBI and CIA may help prevent some acts of terrorism; in fact, since September 2001, more than one hundred potential acts have been thwarted. In *Opposing Viewpoints: Terrorism*, the authors debate some of the issues surrounding terrorism in the following chapters: Is Terrorism a Serious Threat? What Are the Causes of Terrorism? How Should America's Domestic War on Terrorism Be Conducted? How Should the International Community Respond to Terrorism? While terrorism may never be completely eradicated, the United States must not allow the intelligence failures of the past to permit a repeat of September 11.

CHAPTER 1

Is Terrorism a Serious Threat?

Chapter Preface

Terrorism is a problem worldwide, from Colombia, where terrorist groups receive funding from an illicit drug trade, to the Middle East, where Palestinian suicide bombers blow up Israeli restaurants and buses. Since the mid-1990s, Russians have also experienced terrorism, at the hands of Chechen rebels. Although Chechnya declared its independence from Russia in 1991, when the Soviet Union dissolved, and established itself as a republic the following year, Russia has yet to accept Chechnya as an autonomous nation and still views it as a breakaway republic. The struggle between Russia and Chechen rebels, who want Russia to acknowledge Chechnya's independence, has led to an unending cycle in which Chechen rebels commit terrorist acts and Russia retaliates.

Chechen terrorism began in January 1996, following a two-year war for independence from Russia. By the time Russian forces had withdrawn from Chechnya, eighty thousand Chechens had died. When the war ended, Chechnya was still nominally a part of Russia. Two major acts of Chechen terror occurred in the month the war ended, as Chechen rebels aimed to end all ties to Russia. A Turkish Chechen named Muhammed Tokcan took hundreds of cruise line passengers hostage, while at the same time Chechen fighters took the villagers of Pervomaiskoye hostage. The ship's passengers were released four days later, but all the hostages in the village died after a Russian rescue mission failed.

In 1997, the Chechens—who considered themselves essentially independent—elected a president and parliament. That act did not ease tension between Chechnya and Russia, and a second war between Chechen fighters and Russia began in September 1999. Although Russia has still not been able to win that war, despite driving rebels into the Chechen hills, the Kremlin did install a pro-Russian government in Chechnya in January 2001.

Since the beginning of the second war, Chechen terrorism has become increasingly violent. Chechen rebels have received financial support and training from fellow Muslims around the world, including the Saudi Arabian government and the International Islamic Front, which has been associated with terrorist plotter Osama bin Laden. This support and training has had deadly consequences for Russians. Chechen rebels have been suspected of three deadly bombings in Russia in April 2001 and a number of assassinations and abductions of Chechen government officials who support Russia, including seven assassinations between November 2002 and January 2003. The deadliest act of Chechen terrorism occurred in October 2002, when fifty Chechen rebels took hostage approximately 800 people in a Moscow theater. Russian special forces rescued most of the hostages three days later, but the gas the forces used to drive out the rebels killed 129 people. On December 27, 2002, Chechen terrorists blew up the main government building in the capital city of Grozny; that attack killed 72 civilians and wounded 210. Terrorism persisted in 2003, including an August 2003 bombing of a Russian military hospital that left nearly three dozen people dead.

Although Chechen terrorism has been roundly criticized, Russia's response has not been warmly welcomed either. In a January 2003 report, Human Rights Watch criticized the Russian government's use of torture and imprisonment and also contended that Russia's treatment of Chechen civilians—including Chechens not involved in terrorist activity—is genocidal. Neither side appears willing to change its tactics, however, leading to a continued cycle of violence.

The acts of Chechen rebels are but one example of the widespread problem of terrorism. In the following chapters, the authors evaluate the threat of global terrorism. From New York City to Grozny, terrorism is a problem that few people can afford to ignore.

"[Terrorism] is relatively inexpensive to conduct, and devilishly difficult to counter."

Terrorism Poses a Serious Threat

L. Paul Bremer III

In the following viewpoint L. Paul Bremer III argues that the September 11, 2001, attacks on America are an indication of the growing danger of terrorism. He contends that while the number of attacks have declined since the 1970s and 1980s, modern terrorist acts result in higher numbers of casualties. Bremer notes that unlike terrorists from twenty or thirty years ago—who were largely motivated by political beliefs and were loath to alienate the public by killing too many civilians—today's terrorists try to kill as many people as possible in order to call attention to their cause. He maintains that Americans are a favored target of this new brand of terrorism because fanatical terrorists despise the freedom and equality that America represents. Bremer, the former chairman of the National Commission on Terrorism, was appointed by President George W. Bush to lead America's reconstruction efforts in Iraq after the 2003 war there.

As you read, consider the following questions:
1. What were the three pillars of the West's original counterterrorism strategy, as explained by the author?
2. According to Bremer, what two asymmetries are advantageous to terrorists?
3. According to the author, how much did the September 11, 2001, terrorist attacks cost to implement?

"The Third World War was begun on Tuesday, September 11 [2001], on the East Coast of the United States"—so began the French magazine *L'Express* two days later. Whether these words turn out to be prediction or exaggeration will depend on how the world now reacts to the new face of terrorism represented by the vicious attacks of that day.

The September 11 atrocities made for the most dramatic day in American history, dwarfing even the events at Pearl Harbor sixty years ago. Three times as many Americans died in New York and Washington as died at Pearl Harbor. And this time innocent civilians, not military men, were the intended targets. But this was not just an attack on America. Citizens of at least eighty countries died in the collapsed World Trade towers. We are all, in a direct way, victims of the new terrorism.

The Changing Nature of Terrorism

While the attacks were shocking for their audacity and effectiveness, they should have surprised no serious student of terrorism. A large-scale attack on American soil has been widely predicted by experts. For years they have drawn attention to a disturbing paradox: while the number of international terrorist incidents has been declining over the past decade, the number of casualties has risen. This trend reflects the changing motives of terrorists.

During the 1970s and 1980s, most terrorist groups had limited political motives. For them, terrorism was a tactic mainly to draw attention to their "cause." These groups reasoned that many people would sympathize with that cause if only they were made aware of it. Designing their tactics to support this objective, these "old-style" terrorists rarely engaged in indiscriminate mass killing. They rightly concluded such attacks would disgust the very audiences they were trying to convert to their cause. So most terrorist groups designed their attacks to kill enough people to draw in the press but not so many as to repel the public. Often they used terror to force negotiations on some issue, such as the release of jailed comrades. As one terrorism expert put it, these groups were seeking a place at the negotiating table.

Eventually, most terrorist groups in Europe overplayed their hands and the publics turned against them. But antiterrorism policies helped win the day. With vigorous American leadership, European countries and the United States developed a counter-terrorist strategy to deal with this threat. At the heart of that strategy were three principles: make no concessions to terrorists; treat terrorists as criminals to be brought to justice; and punish states that support terrorism. On balance, this strategy worked.

Over the past decade, however, it has become clear that many terrorist groups are motivated less by narrow political goals and more by ideological, apocalyptic or religious fanaticism. Sometimes their goal is simply hatred or revenge, and tactics have changed to reflect these motives. Rather than avoiding large-scale casualties, these terrorists seek to kill as many people as possible. They are unconstrained by the respect for human life that undergirds all the world's great religions, including Islam.

Terrorism Has Become Deadlier

Beginning with the downing of Pan Am Flight 103 in December 1988, through the first World Trade Center bombing in 1993, to the chemical attacks in the Tokyo subways in 1995 and the attacks on two U.S. embassies in East Africa in 1998, terrorist actions have resulted in increasing numbers of casualties. The September 11 attacks killed more than 5,000 people, making it the single worst terrorist attack in world history.[1]

Things could get even worse. During the 1990s, concerns arose that terrorists might use chemical, biological, radiological or nuclear agents. In the 1980s, terrorist groups could have developed such weapons, but they did not do so, apparently calculating that their use would make public support for their causes less likely. But far from steering away from such agents, the new terrorists might find these weapons attractive precisely because they can kill tens of thousands. This was the goal, fortunately unrealized, of Aum Shinrikyo's chemical attack on the Tokyo subway. Indeed, there is evidence that

1. The death toll was later determined to be closer to three thousand.

some new terrorist groups, including [Osama] bin Laden's Al-Qaeda, have tried to acquire nuclear, biological and chemical agents. It is known that the terrorist states of North Korea, Iraq, Iran, Libya and Syria all have tried to develop nuclear, chemical and biological weapons. Moreover, in the 1990s, information about chemical and biological agents became widely available on the Internet. The [fall 2001] anthrax attacks may foreshadow a major escalation to bioterrorism by Islamist and perhaps other terrorists.

The changed motives of these "new-style" terrorists mean that at least two-thirds of the West's old strategy is outmoded. One pillar of that strategy, not making concessions to terrorists, remains valid. But it may be irrelevant when faced with groups like Al-Qaeda. Such groups are not trying to start negotiations. They make no negotiable "demands" that the West can comply with to forestall further attacks. These men do not seek a seat at the table; they want to overturn the table and kill everybody at it.

Misunderstanding Terrorism

It is an honorable reflection of the basic friendliness of the American people that most of us find it difficult to believe that anybody hates Americans. Many find it especially confusing that men who lived among us, sometimes for years, attending our schools and shopping in our malls, should hate the very society whose freedoms they enjoyed. That they somehow must not understand us is the first reaction of many.

But this reaction reflects a misunderstanding about the new terrorists. They hate America precisely because they *do* understand our society; they hate its freedoms, its commitment to equal rights and universal suffrage, its material successes and its appeal to so many non-Americans. Thus, the question of whether or not to make concessions in the face of such hatred is simply irrelevant. Nothing America can say or do, short of ceasing to exist, will satisfy these terrorists.

Our long-standing objective of "bringing terrorists to justice", the second pillar of U.S. strategy, is also irrelevant to the new fight. During the past decade, an increasing percentage of terrorist attacks, especially those conducted by Middle Eastern groups, have involved suicides. This underscores the perpetrators' extraordinary commitment to terror, but it also shows the futility of relying on the concept of using criminal justice to punish them. Men who are prepared to die in an airplane crash are not going to be deterred by the threat of being locked in a prison cell. We need to revise our thinking; now our goal should be, as President [George W.] Bush has suggested, "bringing justice to the terrorists."

Terrorism Is the New Face of War

In the broader sense, the September 11 attacks preview the kind of security threat America will face in the 21st century. Terrorism allows the weak to attack the strong. It is relatively inexpensive to conduct, and devilishly difficult to counter.

Relative to all the other powers in the world, America is stronger than any country has ever been in history. The Gulf War showed that even a lavishly equipped conventional force (at the time, Iraq possessed the world's fifth largest army) was no match for America. The lesson for would-be tyrants and terrorists was clear: America could only be attacked by unconventional means, and terrorism is a fundamental tactic of asymmetrical warfare.

Handelsman. © 2001 by Tribune Media Services. Reproduced by permission.

Terrorists take advantage of two important asymmetries. First, in the fight against terrorism, defenders have to protect all their points of vulnerability around the world; the terrorist has only to attack the weakest point. This lesson was brought home to the U.S. government when Al-Qaeda attacked the American embassies in Nairobi and Dar es-Salaam in August 1998, two embassies thought to be in little danger and thus ill-protected.

Developing Counterterrorist Policy

Secondly, the costs of launching a terrorist attack are a fraction of the costs required to defend against it. To shoot up an airport, a terrorist needs only an AK-47 assault rifle; defending that same airport costs millions of dollars. The September 11 attacks probably cost less than $2 million and caused over $100 billion in damage and business interruption. Thus, the new terrorism reverses the conventional wisdom that, in military operations, the offense must be three times as strong as the defense. . . .

Terrorism Must Be Destroyed

We have seen the face of the new threat to our security in the 21st century. Under Article 51 of the United Nations Charter, the United States is fully justified in taking any and all means of self-defense against that threat. The United States has made clear that it welcomes the assistance of any country in anti-terrorist military operations, and so far the American government has done a masterful job of assembling broad support for the initial phase of the campaign in Afghanistan.[2] The challenge will be to sustain that support as the battle wears on, and especially when the campaign enters the second phase, after we have dealt with Afghanistan.

We must destroy the terrorists before they destroy us. They hate us and are so dangerous that they must be stopped before they can take the battle to a still higher plane of lethality. We must disrupt, dismantle or destroy terrorist groups wherever they are and deny them safe havens. Amer-

---

2. Following the September 11, 2001, attacks the U.S. and coalition forces went to war against the Taliban, the government of Afghanistan that supported the terrorists.

icans should therefore be under no illusions about the campaign we have embarked upon. There will be war with more than one country. As in all wars, there will be civilian casualties. America will win some battles but lose others. More Americans will die. But neither our allies nor our enemies should be in any doubt: We shall prevail.

"We have seen President [George W.] Bush lead a campaign against terrorism that has captured or killed over half of al Qaeda's senior operatives."

The Threat of Terrorism Is Being Reduced

John Ashcroft

In this viewpoint U.S. attorney general John Ashcroft claims that the U.S. government has begun to reduce the threat of terrorism. While Ashcroft acknowledges that terrorism remains a problem, he contends that the coordinated efforts of the Justice Department, law enforcement, and the intelligence community have led to important gains in the war against terrorism, such as the capture or death of senior operatives in the al-Qaeda terrorist organization, the identification of hundreds of suspected terrorists throughout the United States, and the dismantling of the terrorist financial network. Ashcroft asserts that these successes send a message to terrorists that they will be tracked down and brought to justice. This speech was delivered at a Justice Department terrorism roundtable on June 4, 2003.

As you read, consider the following questions:

1. According to the author, from what material is the "gateway to victory" built?
2. What does Ashcroft believe the Justice Department must do if the war on terrorism is to remain successful?
3. According to the attorney general, how many Joint Terrorism Task Forces have been established?

John Ashcroft, opening remarks, Justice Department Terrorism Roundtable, Washington, DC, June 4, 2003.

[On June 3, 2003] we gained three more convictions in the war on terror. This time in the Detroit Cell case: two on terrorist conspiracy charges and the third on visa and document fraud charges.[1]

Learning How to Defeat Terrorism

Victories such as these must be built on a solid foundation: Victory requires vision. Victory requires resolve. But even vision and resolve are useless without men and women of faith and action to carry vision forward.

We have just those kinds of men and women here today.

From across our nation . . . from your hometowns and from our big cities . . . we have gathered together outstanding leaders from our U.S. Attorney's offices who come to share their ideas and their experiences.

If we are to win the war against terrorism, we must learn from the ideas and experiences that have brought us victory and adapt them to defeat our adversaries.

The gateway to victory is built on ideas. We must constantly learn, adapt, outthink, and anticipate the actions of our enemies. We must always be ready to seize the initiative in order to secure victory.

This terrorism roundtable represents the new spirit of cooperation and coordination at the Department of Justice. It gives us the opportunity to discuss proven tactics, to improve teamwork, and to recognize which legal tools work best.

The Efforts of the Department of Justice

Since [the September 11, 2001, terrorist attacks], every agency and every public servant at the Department of Justice has worked to replace a reactive culture of compartmentalization with an assertive and courageous culture of action and results.

By listening and conversing, we have an opportunity to examine the results of our struggle and build on our successes. Over the past 20 months, the Justice Department has

1. The Detroit Cell consisted of four Arab men (one of whom was acquitted) who were charged with working for an unidentified Muslim terrorist organization, raising money, and collecting information on potential terrorist targets.

met and overcome many challenges. We have seen President [George W.] Bush lead a campaign against terrorism that has captured or killed over half of al Qaeda's senior operatives. In the last 20 months, more than 3,000 foot soldiers of terror have been incapacitated.

We gather today recognizing the hard work of the past and also in a spirit of humility. We understand that our work is not yet done and that the future holds yet more challenges to be met and uncertainties to be overcome.

The U.S. Attorneys offices across America have proven themselves over and over to be worthy guardians of freedom. Many of you have dedicated your lives to being career prosecutors for the government. You have executed the Department of Justice's anti-terrorism mission. You have led joint anti-terrorism task forces in the fight to prevent terrorists from striking again.

Slow but Steady

I have said that this is going to be . . . not only a long war, [but] a new kind of war. We're trying to chase down people who hide and move around in the dark corners of the world, and they plot and they plan and then they pop up and kill. They don't care about innocent life. And we're making progress. I mean, we are, slowly but surely, dismantling the al-Qaida [terrorist] network. . . .

And so I'm pleased with progress we've made, but I will continue to warn the American people, like I've been doing for a long time, that this is still a dangerous world we live in.

George W. Bush, remarks at the White House, May 19, 2003.

As President Bush noted, "There is no such thing as perfect security against a hidden network of cold-blooded killers. We're not going to wait until the worst dangers are upon us."

You, your staff, and your colleagues in law enforcement have united with America's intelligence community to share information, to anticipate threats, and to face down the dangers before they are upon us.

Over the past 20 months you and your Justice colleagues have worked with state and local law enforcement, using every legal means to detect, disrupt, and dismantle terrorist networks here and abroad before they strike.

You have respected our Constitutional liberties. You have reflected the moral charge of justice. You have upheld the very rule of law that is so precious to the defense of freedom.

If our war against terrorism is to remain successful, we must constantly adapt and improve our capabilities to protect Americans from a ruthless enemy. Our improved cooperation, coordination and communication on the federal, state and local level must continue.

Proof of Success

Our experience thus far indicates that our coordinated approach is succeeding.

We are gathering and cultivating detailed intelligence on terrorism in the United States:

• Hundreds and hundreds of suspected terrorists have been identified and tracked throughout our nation;

• Our human sources of intelligence have doubled;

• Our counter-terrorism investigations have doubled in one year;

• 18,000 subpoenas and search warrants have been issued; and

• Over 1,000 applications in 2002 were made to the FISA [Foreign Intelligence Surveillance Act] court targeting international terrorists, spies and foreign powers who threaten our security, including 170 emergency FISAs. This is more than 3 times the total number of emergency FISAs obtained in the 23 years prior to September 11th.

We are arresting and detaining potential terrorist threats:

• 4 alleged terrorist cells in Buffalo, Detroit, Seattle and Portland have been broken up;

• 240 individuals have been charged with crimes uncovered in the course of terrorist investigations;

• 129—More than half—have already been convicted or pled guilty, including shoe-bomber Richard Reid, "American Taliban" John Walker Lindh,[2] and the six members of

2. On a December 22, 2001, flight from Paris to Miami, Reid attempted to light a bomb built into his sneakers. His actions were noticed by a flight attendant, and several passengers managed to subdue him, thereby preventing an explosion that would have shattered the plane. Reid admitted having ties to the al Qaeda terrorist network; he was sentenced to life plus thirty years for his crime. Lindh was a

the Buffalo cell, who are cooperating; and

- 515 deportations of illegal aliens linked to the September 11 investigation.

We are dismantling the terrorist financial network:

- 36 designated terrorist organizations;
- Over $125 million in assets frozen and over 600 accounts frozen around the world; and
- 70 investigations into terrorist financing with 23 convictions or guilty pleas to date.

Counter-Terrorism Measures

We are disrupting potential terrorist travel:

- More than 100 airport sweeps in Operation Tarmac with approximately 1,200 arrests for ID and document fraud and other crimes;
- Nine major alien smuggling networks have been disrupted;
- Hundreds of terrorists and criminals have been stopped using the National Security Entry-Exit Registration System (NSEERS) including:
  - 11 suspected terrorists, with at least one known member of al Qaeda;
  - 551 aliens stopped at the border who were wanted criminals, had committed past felonies, or had violated other laws; and
  - 46 felons identified through domestic enrollment, in this country illegally.

We are building a long-term counter-terrorism capacity:

- A near three-fold increase in counter-terrorism funds;
- Over 1,000 new and redirected FBI agents dedicated to counter-terrorism and counter-intelligence;
- We have created positions for 250 new Assistant U.S. Attorneys and established 66 Joint Terrorism Task Forces;
- There has been a 337% increase in Joint Terrorism Task Force staffing; and

twenty-year-old from California who trained in al Qaeda camps and fought with the Taliban (Afghanistan's government, which supported al Qaeda) against American troops and the U.S.-sponsored Northern Alliance. He was detained by U.S. forces and sentenced to twenty years in prison after being convicted of supplying services to the Taliban.

- Fly Away Expert Teams have been organized for world-wide rapid deployment.

These successes send a clear message to terrorists here and abroad: We will find you. We will track you down. We will track down all those who support you. We will not rest until justice is brought to all who would plot against America and strike against the freedom we hold so dear.

I commend each of you for your role in upholding our freedoms and in defending the liberty of generations to come. It is an honor to serve with you.

│*"America's public health establishment must
│ realize that biological weapons exist."*

Biological Terrorism Is a Serious Threat

Scott Gottlieb

In the following viewpoint Scott Gottlieb argues that biological terrorism is a significant threat. He maintains that viruses are especially dangerous because they are easy to produce, can survive outside living cells, and are largely immune to antiviral drugs. Gottlieb further asserts that because smallpox and other viruses can infect thousands of people before they are detected, the United States must develop the ability to detect dangerous microbes before the germs have infected people. Gottlieb is a physician, editor of the *Gilder Biotech Report*, and a columnist for the *American Medical News*.

As you read, consider the following questions:
1. As explained by Gottlieb, what are the two principal forms of disease surveillance?
2. According to the author, what role could computers play in combating bioterrorism?
3. How much time would the nation have to react to a smallpox attack, in Gottlieb's view?

Scott Gottlieb, "Wake Up and Smell the Bio Threat," *American Enterprise*, vol. 14, January/February 2003, pp. 26–27. Copyright © 2003 by American Enterprise Institute for Public Policy Research. Reproduced by permission of The American Enterprise, a magazine of Politics, Business, and Culture. On the web at www.TAEmag.com.

In August 1999, four New York City residents showed up at hospital emergency rooms complaining of headaches and dizziness. A few became paralyzed. Doctors were stumped. Botulism? A rare nerve inflammation? Scans eventually revealed that the patients all had encephalitis—an inflammation of the brain.

Eight cases and another two weeks later, the Centers for Disease Control [CDC] came up with a diagnosis: St. Louis Encephalitis, a viral disease transmitted by mosquitoes. Publicly, the CDC and local health agencies stuck with their diagnosis. Privately, scientists were skeptical: They tested mostly for standard diseases, not rare ones.

CDC scientists continued their research. Doctors didn't crack the case until birds started to die at the Bronx Zoo. An astute veterinarian sent a few bird brains to a friend at the Department of Agriculture. The samples ended up at CDC headquarters in Atlanta, where scientists used genetic fingerprinting to discover that it was West Nile Virus—never before detected in North America—that was making people sick. By autumn, a total of 62 people had been diagnosed with the virus, and six had died.

But less than one of every 100 people infected with West Nile actually becomes seriously ill. Only mosquitoes can spread it. America's next viral outbreak, whether natural or an act of bio-terrorism, may not be so easy on us. The official response to West Nile instills little confidence that disaster could be avoided in the case of a bio-terror attack. Right now, everything America has that was designed specifically to counter bio-terrorism is old, expensive, and slow.

The greatest threat probably comes from viruses: They are relatively easy to engineer into designer bio-weapons. Technicians can produce viruses from a rather small collection of DNA. (In July [2002], scientists reported they had created the polio virus from recipes available on the Internet.) Many viruses can also survive for long periods of time outside living cells, especially in a dry state, where they can easily become airborne. There are no antiviral drugs that have the same striking effectiveness and broad attack range that antibiotics do.

Indeed, we might not even know that an attack had occurred for some time. Most bio-terror experts worry about the silent release of an infectious agent of which we have no hint until the incubation period has passed and the terrorists have fled. Then people would come to emergency rooms with non-specific symptoms that may not immediately trigger the right medical diagnoses. So what's required is a good early warning system. Right now, disease surveillance comes in two principal forms. Passive surveillance usually calls on doctors to take the initiative to report suspicious medical cases to state health authorities. Active surveillance asks public health officials to contact doctors directly to gather the data. Both methods share one inherent handicap: By the time people go to the hospital, an epidemic could have already broken out.

Except for food- and water-borne diseases, the U.S. has no comprehensive system for detecting outbreaks of infectious diseases before people start to get ill. Each state decides which diseases to report to the state health department and which information to pass on to the CDC. Often, chaos results. "There's so much noise, we can hardly pick up the signal," says Frederick Burkle of the Defense Threat Reduction Agency at Johns Hopkins University. Even worse, we don't even have the needed technology: About half of state labs can't do the type of genetic testing that ultimately unearthed West Nile.

A New Type of Surveillance

A bit of progress has been made: The CDC is encouraging local public health leaders to develop systems for surveying the public for worrisome signs such as unusual diagnoses or spikes in doctor visits—a practice public health officials call syndromic surveillance. New York City has such a system in place: Emergency rooms feed data into a central computer system; software alerts public health officials when it finds clusters of symptoms in one geographic area, unusual combinations of symptoms, or inordinately high numbers of symptoms reported by a particular hospital. Health officials hope to couple these systems with databases that track over-the-counter drug sales (patients often purchase medicine before they decide to go to the emergency room).

Syndromic surveillance is swiftly becoming a mainstay of bio-terror preparedness nationwide. It has also prompted a rash of false alarms, as doctors, trained to spot these syndromes, leap to conclusions they would never have considered before 9/11. On August 4, an emergency room doctor at Beth Israel Hospital in Brooklyn decided that a patient with fever and a skin rash fit the description for smallpox. He activated New York's emergency response system over what turned out to be a mild case of contact dermatitis.

The Greatest Threats

The biggest biological threats, according to the Centers for Disease Control:

• **Anthrax:** Starts with flulike symptoms; lethal without antibiotics

• **Smallpox:** Starts with fever, aches, vomiting; progresses to body blisters; often fatal

• **Pneumonic plague:** Symptoms include fever, chills and cough; without early treatment, causes breathing trouble and death

• **Botulinum toxin:** This toxin, often the culprit in food poisoning, can cause blurry vision, then whole-body paralysis that can last for months

• **Tularemia:** Inhaling this bacteria can cause fever and a pneumonialike illness: rarely fatal, particularly when treated with antibiotics

• **Filoviruses:** Ebola and other filoviruses cause fever and internal bleeding; rapidly fatal and no treatment is available

• **Arenaviruses:** Lassa fever and other arenaviruses cause symptoms that include fever and vomiting; usually not fatal with treatment

Centers for Disease Control and Prevention, 2001.

And there is much skepticism about the approach. "Syndromic diagnosis—that's nothing but a big charade," says Dr. C.J. Peters, former head of the CDC's top security lab. "By the time you start getting blips in emergency rooms, it's too late."

President [George W.] Bush has pledged $11 billion [between 2003 and 2004] to reconfigure the infrastructure of the national health system. The federal government has already spent more than $3 billion to upgrade disease surveillance, expand laboratories, and improve communications abilities. But all of these measures won't much strengthen our ability to detect unusual microbes.

A National Trip-Wire

Health officials still focus on tracking downstream markers of disease, the things that happen after people get sick—medicine purchases, strange clinical syndromes, doctor visits. Instead, surveillance systems need to be geared to spotting the microbes themselves, before people have incubated and spread these germs. Some scientists want to develop means for routinely screening blood for the myriad viruses ranging from influenza to designer bugs terrorists might develop. If this kind of surveillance existed, it could provide a national trip-wire for new viral pathogens.

How would it work? Health officials would collect samples of serum from all the blood that ordinary diagnostic labs dispose of daily. A national lab would screen the samples for viruses. That way, health officials could detect infections before people develop symptoms, allowing for quarantines and early medical interventions to control impending epidemics.

This idea is the brainchild of Norman Anderson, a celebrated researcher in vaccine purification and clinical testing who heads the Viral Defense Foundation, and his son Leigh Anderson, the former chief scientific officer at the biotech firm Large Scale Biology. The technology already exists to sequence viruses' DNA—a technique called shotgun sequencing. It was pioneered by Craig Venter, the former chief executive of Celera Genomics, which mapped the human genome in record time, and has become the mainstay of genomic research. The Andersons' proposal would involve checking each blood sample for viruses and then comparing them to a computer database of known viruses around the world. (It's a similar technique that ultimately led scientists to discover that West Nile Virus was behind the deaths in New York.) Computers could keep count of what has been found in a particular blood sample, and assemble a human virus index to monitor the ebb and flow of different diseases in the population. Any DNA sequences that the computer didn't recognize could be flagged for bio-terrorism monitors. If this technology sounds futuristic, it's not. Oceanic researchers already employ similar procedures to separate viruses from ocean water.

To get a representative sample, researchers would probably need to take blood only from a select group of labs, not all of them. Right now, CDC researchers call up a pre-selected group of doctors scattered across the country to check for any unusual medical cases. This system relies on doctors to spot the early signs and symptoms of something more sinister than ordinary influenza. West Nile proved this kind of surveillance slow, and too unreliable to thwart outbreaks. By going straight to blood, the CDC can have early and incontrovertible data.

A Looming Threat

Alas, public health officials by their very training are averse to such technological solutions, placing their faith in statistics and epidemiology. But these techniques suffer from poor sensitivity, lack of timeliness, and minimal coverage. America's public health establishment must realize that biological weapons exist. As biology moves from a laboratory to a digital science, even unsophisticated hacks can develop dangerous weapons. As terrorists bring increasing sophistication to their craft there's a growing disproportion between our defensive technologies—developed to thwart ordinary illnesses—and the bio-weapons.

The threat of smallpox looms large right now, and policymakers are debating how many vaccine doses to make available. Iraq and North Korea, among others, probably have smallpox samples that could be turned into weapons. If smallpox were released into our cities, officials might have only a few hours to react. By the time the virus is first detected, it could have already spread to hundreds or thousands of close contacts. Sick people will have boarded planes to distant locations, coughed their way through closed buildings, or ridden on subways. That's how pandemics start.

"Bio-chem hype . . . is being used to justify a variety of questionable public policy proposals."

The Threat of Biological Terrorism Has Been Exaggerated

Jim Walsh

The media and American politicians have overhyped the danger of biological and chemical attacks, Jim Walsh claims in the following viewpoint. Walsh argues that terrorist groups have never used biological weapons, and the sole chemical attack killed only twelve people. He maintains that the rhetoric of Attorney General John Ashcroft and irresponsible television news stories have dangerous consequences, from needlessly scaring Americans to actually encouraging terrorist groups to use these weapons. Jim Walsh is the director of the Managing the Atom Project and a research fellow at the Belfer Center for Science and International Affairs at Harvard University.

As you read, consider the following questions:

1. According to Walsh, how were biological weapons used in colonial America?
2. How does the author describe the typical television story on biochemical terrorism?
3. In the author's opinion, what steps should the Bush administration take to reduce the possibility of a biological or chemical attack?

Jim Walsh, "Bio-Chem Hype Spreads Like a New Form of Infectious Disease," *Los Angeles Times*, October 5, 2001, p. B15. Copyright © 2001 by the *Los Angeles Times*. Reproduced by permission.

There's something in the air, and it is spreading. You can't walk down a street or go to work without being exposed. Worse yet, it's reaching your kids. It's not a chemical or biological agent. It's fear.

It is, however, a fear all out of proportion to reality. It is fear based on hype, and sadly, some of the hype is driven by parochial interest. [An October 2001] report of an isolated case of anthrax will only make things worst.

The Facts About Bio-Chemical Terrorism

First, consider the facts. Chemical weapons have been with us since World War I. Biological weapons have an even longer history, stretching back centuries to the Peloponnesian War and, more famously, to early America when Indian tribes were supplied with blankets infected with smallpox. Despite this long history, biological and chemical weapons have rarely been used, and then only by countries. No country, however, would attack the U.S. with such weapons for fear of nuclear retaliation. There has not been a single death due to a bio-attack by terrorists.

Casualties from a terrorist chemical attack are almost as rare. Only once has a terrorist group used chemical weapons to deadly effect—the 1995 attack by the Aum Supreme Truth, a Japanese cult. Even in that case, the attack was more failure than success; 12 people were killed in a crowded Tokyo subway. Had they used a traditional high explosive, the death toll would have been far greater. Many warned that Aum's attack would set off a wave of chemical attacks. That didn't happen.

Politicians and the media would have us believing the worst. Atty. Gen. John Ashcroft, who threw the city of Boston into a panic [on September 21, 2001] when he warned of a possible attack, continues to use inflammatory rhetoric about chemical-biological terrorism. His aides admit that there is no new intelligence to substantiate such claims. His warnings seem to coincide with testimony aimed at getting passage of sweeping new anti-terrorism laws.

Defense Secretary Donald Rumsfeld is a little more cautious. He claims that terrorists will eventually acquire such weapons from countries. What he fails to mention is that no country has ever provided a weapon of mass destruction to a terrorist group. They do not give them to groups over which they have limited control and which might use the weapons against them later.

Too Much Media Hype

The media treatment of bio-chem terrorism has been predictable and regrettable. This is particularly true of television, which cannot resist showing images of gas masks and exploding canisters. The typical story begins with dire warnings about the consequences of a perfectly executed chemical or biological attack. This is followed by interviews with public health officials who solemnly declare that the U.S. is unprepared for such an attack. Only at the very end is the viewer told that the risk of such an attack is exceedingly small. By then the damage is done.

Anthrax Is Difficult to Spread

It is not the single death from anthrax that really worries us but the unknown possibility of a full-scale bioterror attack. But here we need to rationally consider the risk of a large attack and the likely harm it will cause. It takes a great deal of sophistication to generate the right-sized spores and, even more challenging, the right way of aerosolizing them over a large area. Spiked letters are not terribly effective at spreading anthrax to thousands, let alone millions, of people.

Ezekiel J. Emanuel, *Wall Street Journal*, October 22, 2001.

If bio-chem threats are being hyped, why aren't there more voices of caution? There are two reasons. First, there is no cost to being a Cassandra. If the dire predictions do not come true, the analyst simply can say that we have been lucky. By contrast, the person who suggests that the threats are overblown is taking a career-threatening risk. One attack—even if it fails, even if it employs a household cleaner rather than sarin or anthrax—would be viewed as having proved the skeptic wrong.

There is a second, less obvious reason. There is an unwritten rule among the small fraternity of people who study weapons of mass destruction. When colleagues engage in hype, many of us will turn a deaf ear rather than publicly contradict them. We tell ourselves that hyping the threat is the only way to get the attention of the U.S. public and therefore a necessary evil.

[The September 11, 2001, terrorist attacks] changed all that. Today, bio-chem hype has real consequences. It is needlessly scaring our children. It is being used to justify a variety of questionable public policy proposals, and worse, it may actually encourage terrorists to consider these weapons.

The Disease of Fear

Yes, we should reduce the danger of a biological or chemical attack. We can improve the public health infrastructure and, in particular, the worldwide monitoring of infectious disease. We can work on vaccines and techniques to prevent advances in the lab from becoming new weapons. Finally, the Bush administration should reverse course and support the chemical weapons and the biological weapons treaties, which aim to reduce the risks of biological and chemical warfare.

The infectious disease gripping the U.S. is fear. Left untreated, this disease may have disastrous consequences—for public policy, for the economy and for our daily lives and the lives of our children.

*"The U.S. is the only country that was
condemned for international terrorism by
the World Court."*

America Is a Serious Terrorist Threat

Noam Chomsky, interviewed by David Barsamian

The United States is responsible for numerous acts of terrorism, Noam Chomsky argues in the following viewpoint. He asserts that the federal government has a long history of supporting terrorism in Afghanistan and Israel. Chomsky also claims that the United States has not only abetted terrorists but also committed its own attacks, including bombings in Lebanon and Sudan. Chomsky is a political activist, professor of linguistics at the Massachusetts Institute of Technology, and the author of numerous books and articles, including *World Orders Old and New* and *The New Military Humanism*. David Barsamian is the founder and director of Alternative Radio and a writer whose books include *Propaganda and the Public Mind: Conversations with Noam Chomsky*.

As you read, consider the following questions:
1. According to Chomsky, how do wealthy Muslims view the United States?
2. How many Lebanese died in a 1985 truck bombing authorized by the Reagan administration, according to the author?
3. How does Chomsky define terrorism?

Noam Chomsky, interviewed by David Barsamian, "The United States Is a Leading Terrorist State," *Monthly Review*, vol. 53, November 2001. Copyright © 1993 by MR Press. Reproduced by permission of Monthly Review Foundation.

*D*avid Barsamian: *The media have been noticeably lacking in providing a context and a background for the [September 11, 2001] attacks on New York and Washington. What might be some useful information that you could provide?*

Noam Chomsky: There are two categories of information that are particularly useful because there are two distinct, though related, sources for the attack. Let's assume that the attack was rooted somehow in the bin Laden network.[1] That sounds plausible, at least, so let's say it's right. If that's right, there are two categories of information and of populations that we should be concerned with, linked but not identical. One is the bin Laden network. That's a category by itself. Another is the population of the region. They're not the same thing, although there are links. What ought to be in the forefront is discussion of both of those. The bin Laden network, I doubt if anybody knows it better than the CIA, since they were instrumental in helping construct it.[2] This is a network whose development started in 1979, if you can believe President [Jimmy] Carter's National Security Advisor Zbigniew Brzezinski. He claimed, maybe he was just bragging, that in mid-1979 he had instigated secret support for Mujahedin fighting against the government of Afghanistan in an effort to draw the Russians into what he called an "Afghan trap," a phrase worth remembering. He's very proud of the fact that they did fall into the Afghan trap by sending military forces to support the government six months later, with consequences that we know. The U.S., along with Egypt, Pakistan, French intelligence, Saudi Arabian funding, and Israeli involvement, assembled a major army, a huge mercenary army, maybe 100,000 or more, and they drew from the most militant sectors they could find, which happened to be radical Islamists, what are called here Islamic fundamentalists, from all over, most of them not from Afghanistan. They're called Afghanis, but like bin Laden, they come from elsewhere.

1. Osama bin Laden and his terrorist organization al Qaeda were believed to be the perpetrators of the September 11, 2001, attacks on the United States. 2. During the Soviet Union's occupation of Afghanistan in the 1980s, the CIA funded the training of bin Laden and other Afghanis, which many people believe provided bin Laden with skills that would later prove useful as he built up a terrorist network.

Bin Laden joined very quickly. He was involved in the funding networks, which probably are the ones which still exist. They were trained, armed, organized by the CIA, Pakistan, Egypt, and others to fight a holy war against the Russians. And they did. They fought a holy war against the Russians. They carried terror into Russian territory. They may have delayed the Russian withdrawal, a number of analysts believe, but they did win the war and the Russian invaders withdrew. The war was not their only activity. In 1981, groups based in that same network assassinated President [Anwar] Sadat of Egypt, who had been instrumental in setting it up. In 1983, one suicide bomber, maybe with connections to the same networks, essentially drove the U.S. military out of Lebanon. And it continued. By 1989, they had succeeded in their holy war in Afghanistan. As soon as the U.S. established a permanent military presence in Saudi Arabia, bin Laden and the rest announced that from their point of view this was comparable to the Russian occupation of Afghanistan and they turned their guns on the Americans, as had already happened in 1983 when the U.S. had military forces in Lebanon. Saudi Arabia is a major enemy of the bin Laden network, just as Egypt is. That's what they want to overthrow, what they call the un-Islamic governments of Egypt, Saudi Arabia, other states of the Middle East and North Africa. And it continued.

In 1997, they murdered roughly sixty tourists in Egypt and destroyed the Egyptian tourist industry. And they've been carrying out activities all over the region, North Africa, East Africa, the Middle East, for years. That's one group. And that is an outgrowth of the U.S. wars of the 1980s and, if you can believe Brzezinski, even before, when they set the "Afghan trap." There's a lot more to say about them, but that's one part. Another is the people of the region. They're connected, of course. The bin Laden network and others like them draw a lot of their support from the desperation and anger and resentment of the people of the region, which ranges from rich to poor, secular to radical Islamist. The *Wall Street Journal*, to its credit, has run a couple of articles on attitudes of wealthy Muslims, the people who most interest them: businessmen, bankers, professionals, and others through the Middle East region who are very frank about their grievances. They put it more politely than the poor people in the slums and the streets, but it's clear. Everybody knows what they are. For one thing, they're very angry about U.S. support for undemocratic, repressive regimes in the region and U.S. insistence on blocking any efforts towards democratic openings. You just heard on the news, it sounded like the BBC, a report that the Algerian government is now interested in getting involved in [the war against the Taliban government in Afghanistan]. The announcer said that there had been plenty of Islamic terrorism in Algeria, which is true, but he didn't tell the other part of the story, which is that a lot of the terrorism is apparently state terrorism. There's pretty strong evidence for that. The government of course is interested in enhancing its repression, and will welcome U.S. assistance in this.

Supporting Israeli Occupation

In fact, that government is in office because it blocked the democratic election in which it would have lost to mainly Islamic-based groups. That set off the current fighting. Similar things go on throughout the region. The "moneyed Muslims" interviewed by the *Journal* also complained that the U.S. has blocked independent economic development by "propping up oppressive regimes," that's the phrase they used. But the prime concern stressed in the *Wall Street Journal* articles and by everybody who knows anything about the region, the prime concern of the "moneyed Muslims"—basically pro-American, incidentally—is the dual U.S. policies, which contrast very sharply in their eyes, towards Iraq and Israel. In the case of Iraq, for the last ten years the U.S. and Britain have been devastating the civilian society. [Former secretary of state] Madeleine Albright's infamous statement about how maybe half a million children have died, and it's a high price but we're willing to pay it, doesn't sound too good among people who think that maybe it matters if a half a million children are killed by the U.S. and Britain. And meanwhile they're strengthening [Iraqi leader] Saddam Hussein. So that's one aspect of the dual policy. The other aspect is that the U.S. is the prime supporter of the Israeli military occupation of Palestinian territory, now in its thirty-fifth year. It's been harsh and brutal from the beginning, extremely repressive. Most of this hasn't been discussed here, and the U.S. role has been virtually suppressed. It goes back twenty-five years of blocking diplomatic initiatives.

A "Rogue State"

The U.S. today . . . has the greatest arsenal of conventional and nuclear weapons. Indeed, [President George W.] Bush recently announced plans to restart nuclear testing. The U.S conducts biological warfare in Colombia, spraying dangerous fungi (the use of which is banned in the U.S.) over vast areas to destroy illegal drug crops, and it is currently developing allegedly nonlethal weapons to be used for "crowd control":

> The weapons include publicized items such as microwaves to heat the skin, sound generators to vibrate human internal organs, and lasers to overwhelm the senses.
>
> Cloaked in greater secrecy are investigations into chemical and biological weapons. The Joint Non-Lethal Weapons Program (JNLWP) has entertained proposals to use sedatives, calmatives, opioids . . . foul smelling substances, muscle relaxants, and other drugs on "potentially hostile civilians" (and combatants). JNLWP has weighted genetically engineered microbes to disable enemy vehicles and machinery or to destroy supplies. Delivery mechanisms studied include backpack sprayers, land mines and binary weapons, mid-air exploding mortar shells for riot control, and as payloads in unmanned aerial vehicles.

The U.S. maintains, says [Edward] Hammond [director of a biological weapons watchdog group], "far and away the largest biological weapons defense program in the world," prompting some international critics to "convincingly argue the U.S. is a chemical and biological weapons control 'rogue state.'" [In July 2003] the U.S. deliberately scuttled verification of the Biological and Toxin Weapons Convention, setting back six years of negotiations in order to protect its secret CIA biological weapons programs from international scrutiny.

Joe Allen, *International Socialist Review*, January/February 2002.

Even simple facts are not reported. For example, as soon as the current fighting began last September 30 [2001], Israel immediately, the next day, began using U.S. helicopters (they can't produce helicopters) to attack civilian targets. In the next couple of days they killed several dozen people in apartment complexes and elsewhere. The fighting was all in the occupied territories, and there was no Palestinian fire. The Palestinians were using stones. So this is people throwing stones against occupiers in a military occupation, legitimate resistance by world standards, insofar as the targets are military.

On October 3 [2000], [President Bill] Clinton made the biggest deal in a decade to send new military helicopters to Israel. That continued the next couple of months. That wasn't even reported, still isn't reported, as far as I'm aware. But the people there know it, even if they don't read the Israeli press (where it was immediately reported). They look in the sky and see attack helicopters coming and they know they're U.S. attack helicopters sent with the understanding that that is how they will be used. From the very start U.S. officials made it clear that there were no conditions on their use, which was by then already well known. A couple of weeks later Israel started using them for assassinations. The U.S. issued some reprimands but sent more helicopters, the most advanced in the U.S. arsenal. Meanwhile the settlement policies, which have taken over substantial parts of the territories and are designed to make it virtually impossible for a viable independent state to develop, are supported by the U.S. The U.S. provides the funding, the diplomatic support. It's the only country that's blocked the overwhelming international consensus on condemning all this under the Geneva conventions. The victims, and others in the region, know all of this. All along this has been an extremely harsh military occupation. . . .

America's Terrorist Acts

Your [view] that the U.S. is a "leading terrorist state" might stun many Americans. Could you elaborate on that? . . .

The U.S. is the only country that was condemned for international terrorism by the World Court and that rejected a Security Council resolution calling on states to observe international law. It continues international terrorism. Violent assaults in Nicaragua are the least of it. And there are also what are in comparison, minor examples. Everybody here was quite properly outraged by the Oklahoma City bombing,[3] and for a couple of days, the headlines all read, Oklahoma City looks like Beirut. I didn't see anybody point out that Beirut also looks like Beirut, and part of the reason is that the Reagan Administration had set off a terrorist bombing there in 1985 that was very much like Oklahoma City, a truck bombing outside a mosque timed to kill the maximum number of people as they left. It killed eighty and wounded two hundred, aimed at a Muslim cleric whom they didn't like and whom they missed. It was not very secret. I don't know what name you give to the attack that's killed maybe a million civilians in Iraq and maybe a half a million children, which is the price the Secretary of State says we're willing to pay. Is there a name for that? Supporting Israeli atrocities is another one. Supporting Turkey's crushing of its own Kurdish population, for which the Clinton Administration gave the decisive support, 80 percent of the arms, escalating as atrocities increased, is another. Or take the bombing of the Sudan, one little footnote, so small that it is casually mentioned in passing in reports on the background to the Sept. 11 crimes. How would the same commentators react if the bin Laden network blew up half the pharmaceutical supplies in the U.S. and the facilities for replenishing them? Or Israel? Or any country where people "matter"? Although that's not a fair analogy, because the U.S. target is a poor country which had few enough drugs and vaccines to begin with and can't replenish them. Nobody knows how many thousands or tens of thousands of deaths resulted from that single atrocity, and bringing up that death toll is considered scandalous. If somebody did that to the U.S. or its allies, can you imagine the reaction? In this case we say, Oh, well, too bad, minor mistake, let's go on to the next topic. Other people in the world don't react like that. When bin Laden brings up that bombing, he strikes a resonant chord, even with people who despise and fear him, and the same, unfortunately, is true of much of the rest of his rhetoric.

Or to return to "our own little region over here," as [for-

3. On April 19, 1995, a car bomb exploded outside the federal office building in Oklahoma City, killing 168 people. It was the worst terrorist attack on American soil until September 11, 2001. Timothy McVeigh and Terry Nichols were convicted for their role in the bombing, with McVeigh receiving the death penalty.

mer secretary of war] Henry Stimson called it, take Cuba. After many years of terror beginning in late 1959, including very serious atrocities, Cuba should have the right to resort to violence against the U.S. according to U.S. doctrine that is scarcely questioned. It is, unfortunately, all too easy to continue, not only with regard to the U.S. but also other terrorist states. . . .

The Politics of Terrorism

National Public Radio, which in the 1980s was denounced by the Reagan Administration as "Radio Managua on the Potomac," is also considered out there on the liberal end of respectable debate. Noah Adams, the host of "All Things Considered," asked these questions on September 17 [2001]. Should assassinations be allowed? Should the CIA be given more operating leeway?

The CIA should not be permitted to carry out assassinations, but that's the least of it. Should the CIA be permitted to organize a car bombing in Beirut like the one I described? Not a secret, incidentally; prominently reported in the mainstream media, though easily forgotten. That didn't violate any laws. And it's not just the CIA. Should they have been permitted to organize in Nicaragua a terrorist army which had the official task, straight out of the mouth of the State Department, to attack "soft targets," meaning undefended agricultural cooperatives and health clinics? What's the name for that? Or to set up something like the bin Laden network, not him himself but the background networks? Should the U.S. be authorized to provide Israel with attack helicopters to carry out political assassinations and attacks on civilian targets? That's not the CIA. That's the Clinton Administration, with no noticeable objection, in fact, even reported.

Could you very briefly define the political uses of terrorism? Where does it fit in the doctrinal system?

The U.S. is officially committed to what is called "low-intensity warfare." That's the official doctrine. If you read the definition of low-intensity conflict in army manuals and compare it with official definitions of "terrorism" in army manuals, or the U.S. Code, you find they're almost the same. Terrorism is the use of coercive means aimed at civilian populations in an effort to achieve political, religious, or other aims. That's what the World Trade Center bombing [on September 11, 2001] was, a particularly horrifying terrorist crime. And that's official doctrine. I mentioned a couple of examples. We could go on and on. It's simply part of state action, not just the U.S. of course. Furthermore, all of these things should be well known. It's shameful that they're not. Anybody who wants to find out about them can begin by reading a collection of essays published ten years ago by a major publisher called *Western State Terrorism*, edited by Alex George (Routledge, 1991), which runs through lots and lots of cases. These are things people need to know if they want to understand anything about themselves. They are known by the victims of course, but the perpetrators prefer to look elsewhere.

"The bombing in Bali . . . reflected a desire on the part of many fundamentalist Muslims to quell the constant intrusion of Western influences."

Southeast Asian Terrorism Is a Serious Problem

Llewellyn D. Howell

The October 2002 bombing of Bali nightclubs illustrates the growing danger posed by Southeast Asian terrorists, Llewellyn D. Howell maintains in the following viewpoint. He argues that the bombing, which killed 190 people, sent a message that Westerners are vulnerable to attacks in any nation that has a radical Islamic population. Howell further claims that these terrorist acts will devastate the economies of Bali and other culturally diverse Southeast Asian nations, as Western tourists opt not to endanger themselves by visiting these countries. Howell is the international affairs editor of *USA Today* magazine.

As you read, consider the following questions:
1. How has Hindu culture made Bali a popular tourist destination, in Howell's opinion?
2. What were the results of the Association of Southeast Asian Nations summit, according to Howell?
3. According to the author, how much money did Indonesia generate from tourism in 2001?

The October 12, 2002, bombing of nightclubs in Bali has turned the world of travel and tourism in Southeast Asia upside down. Bali had always been an island of tranquility in Indonesia. Its history dates to the powerful Madjapahit empire that existed from 1100 to 1500 A.D. on eastern Java and the adjacent islands. The Madjapahit political dynasty traced its origins to the Indian Hindu polities that led to the development of all Southeast Asian states except Vietnam. Most of Madjapahit was eventually subjugated to the expanding Islamic empires that followed the founding of Malacca in 1400 A.D., but Bali escaped with its Hindu culture intact.

It is that Hindu culture that has made Bali the most-attractive vacation site in the region for the last half-century. The more-permissive atmosphere of Hinduism allowed sun-bathing, partying, and general relaxing by Australians, Europeans, and Americans that didn't fit the local culture in the rest of Islamic Indonesia. The hotels and resorts of Bali have been bringing hundreds of millions of dollars steadily into foreign currency–starved Indonesia for decades.

A Strike Against the West

The bombing in Bali killed more than 190, mostly Australians, but others as well, including seven Americans, in a tactical hit for the terrorists' cause. It was also a strategic strike at the heart of Indonesia and the region. It reflected a desire on the part of many fundamentalist Muslims to quell the constant intrusion of Western influences into the country and incidentally served to send a message to the Hindu population of the island. Where Bali's domestic population gained from the interaction with the flow of tourism, there has been a leveling to the least common denominator. Jakarta's Center for Labor and Development estimates that 150,000 tourism-related jobs will be lost on Bali and close to 1,000,000 for Indonesia as a whole.

The bombing was a powerful message across the region. Those nations with fundamentalist and radical Islamic populations—whether in large numbers or small minorities—are now deemed physically vulnerable to attacks on Westerners. These states include Indonesia, Malaysia, Thailand,

Brunei, Singapore, and the Philippines. The U.S., Australia, and Great Britain have issued warnings to their citizens about visiting these countries and, if they do, about avoiding groups and some locations.

There have been sufficient departures and trip cancellations that the meeting of the heads of state of the Association of Southeast Asian Nations in November [2002] began with a focus on the devastating effect the drop in tourism revenue is having. The two-day summit of the 10 heads of state resulted in pledges of further cooperation among law enforcement bodies to protect visitors and investors, and the establishment of an antiterrorism center to be located in Malaysia, but these measures are probably too late.

The Lessons of Terror

The lessons of the Bali explosions for the tourism industry have compounded those already provided by attacks by Islamic radicals on tourists at Luxor and other sites in Egypt, Algeria, Sabah, Malaysia, and the southern Philippines. The lessons are, first, that Western tourists are viable targets for terrorists. Second, the danger is global, and no country or location is immune. Third, Islamic populations are the source of active terrorism. While the war on terrorism may not be a war against Islam, there is a very high correlation between attacks on tourists and instigation by Islamic terrorists, rather than Hindu, Buddhist, or Christian. No amount of political correctness can disguise this fact from tourists, tour organizers, and insurance companies.

Fourth, culturally diverse societies—if one of the subcultures is Muslim—are likely to be hot spots for Western tourists. This is critical to the tourism industry since the culturally diverse destinations have been the most-interesting ones. Fifth, open societies that allow unrestricted internal travel are more vulnerable to terrorist attacks. Hence, the strength of the tourism case for countries like Vietnam that have tight controls over the practice of religion and travel into and within the country. There is a small Muslim population there, but all religions function under a restrictive official institution sanctioned by the central government.

As tourism suffers through the reaction to danger and

deaths, the fear factor infects other industries as well. Bali garment-makers are concerned that buyers will not arrive as scheduled to place orders for 2003. If that industry falters, employment could greatly diminish, since one-eighth of the island's population have textile-related jobs. Nike has confirmed plans to shift most of its shoe production lines from Indonesia to Vietnam. Businesses that have no portability—such as Exxon Mobile in northern Sumatra and Freeport McMoran Copper and Gold in West Papua at the other end of Indonesia—have had to step up security, adding considerable cost to their extraction products and, ultimately, reducing income for the countries in which they are operating.

A History of Violence

[Terrorism] is not new to Indonesia. First, the military takeover in the mid-1960s that brought the Suharto regime to power, cost the lives of hundreds of thousands of people. They were presumed to be communists and so were killed or died in prison. The exact figure will never be known. The military maintained their central role in all aspects of Indonesian life. There was no democracy. Instead of general elections, they simply had elections of generals. Three decades later, when the Suharto regime started to collapse, over a thousand lives were lost in riots in May 1998 alone. . . . [Also] there are various terrorist groups at work in Indonesia and the neighbouring countries. For example, Jemaah Islamiah (JI) seeks to create an Islamic state consisting of Singapore, Malaysia, the southern Philippines and parts of Indonesia. 80 per cent of the national borders around the world were created by Europeans in the last 500 years of European imperialism. JI does not recognize the European boundaries and so seeks to fashion its own state.

But JI is just one of several Islamic fundamentalist groups in the south-east Asian region using violence. The southern Philippines-based Moro Liberation Front and Abu Sayyaf, for example, have also committed terrorist crimes, including the killing of foreign tourists. Striking at one terrorist group alone will not solve the problem because others will arise.

Keith Suter, *Contemporary Review*, January 2003.

It is the ultimate irony. Those who have argued that the wave of terrorism over the last decade has its roots in poverty and economic disparity now see a far-greater negative impact of terrorist actions on those societies than elsewhere. Tourism is Indonesia's third-largest industry after oil and textiles. It generated nearly $5,500,000,000 in 2001. J.P. Morgan forecasts that up to $3,000,000,000 in tourism revenues will be lost in the year following the Bali attack and that 2003 economic growth will be cut by nearly one percent, a loss that poverty-stricken Indonesia cannot afford. The attacks on tourists have become as much an assault on the societies that host them as on Western visitors.

Ironic, too, is the fact that the countries that will benefit from the attacks—in tourism revenues and direct investment—are repressive societies like Vietnam that control their religions and populations. In this very odd twist, what were the risks of the recent past have become very attractive alternatives in a world filled with danger, but one that is also seeing an exponential growth in interest and financial capability on the part of would-be sightseers and students of the human condition.

"The link between drugs and terrorism is not a new phenomenon."

Narcoterrorism Is a Serious Threat

Steven W. Casteel

In the following viewpoint, originally given as testimony before the Senate Committee on the Judiciary on May 20, 2003, Steven W. Casteel asserts that narcoterrorism—when terrorism is funded by the sale of illegal drugs—is a worldwide threat. He contends that narcoterrorism is a particularly serious problem throughout South America, where terrorist organizations such as Colombia's National Liberation Army use profits from cocaine and heroin trafficking to help finance car bombings, kidnappings, assassinations, and other terrorist acts. According to Casteel, narcoterrorism will persist until the flow of drug money is stopped. Casteel is an assistant administrator for intelligence for the Drug Enforcement Administration.

As you read, consider the following questions:
1. What is the Drug Enforcement Administration's mission, as stated by Casteel?
2. According to the author, how do the Revolutionary Armed Forces of Colombia utilize their relationships with global smuggling operations?
3. In Casteel's opinion, what did the September 11, 2001, terrorist attacks "graphically illustrate"?

Steven W. Casteel, testimony before the Senate Committee on the Judiciary, May 20, 2003.

Prior to [the September 11, 2001, terrorist attacks] the law enforcement community typically addressed drug trafficking and terrorist activities as separate issues. In the wake of the terrorist attacks in New York City, Washington, DC, and Pennsylvania, these two criminal activities are visibly intertwined. For the Drug Enforcement Administration (DEA), investigating the link between drugs and terrorism has taken on renewed importance. More importantly, it has heightened the visibility of DEA's mission—one that was present even before September 11th.

A Long-Standing Link Between Drugs and Terror

Throughout history, a broad spectrum of the criminal element—from drug traffickers to arms smugglers to terrorists—have used their respective power and profits in order to instill the fear and corruption required to shield them from the law. Perhaps the most recognizable illustration of this linkage is the expansion of traditional organized crime in the United States during the early 20th century. Whether a group is committing terrorist acts, trafficking drugs or laundering money, the one constant to remember is that they are all forms of organized crime. The links between various aspects of the criminal world are evident because those who use illicit activities to further or fund their lifestyle, cause, or fortune often interact with others involved in related illicit activities. For example, organizations that launder money for drug traffickers often utilize their existing infrastructure to launder money for arms traffickers, terrorists, etc. The link between drugs and terrorism is not a new phenomenon.

Globalization has dramatically changed the face of both legitimate and illegitimate enterprise. Criminals, by exploiting advances in technology, finance, communications, and transportation in pursuit of their illegal endeavors, have become criminal entrepreneurs. Perhaps the most alarming aspect of this "entrepreneurial" style of crime is the intricate manner in which drugs and terrorism may be intermingled. Not only is the proliferation of illegal drugs perceived as a danger, but the proceeds from the sale of drugs provides a ready source of funding for other criminal activities, including terrorism.

Chairman [Orrin] Hatch, Ranking Member [Patrick] Leahy and distinguished members of the [Senate Judiciary] committee, it is my distinct pleasure to appear before you in my capacity as the Assistant Administrator for Intelligence of the DEA. Before I begin, Mr. Chairman, I would like to recognize you and the members of the committee for your outstanding support of DEA's mission and the men and women who serve it.

The DEA does not specifically target terrorists or terrorist organizations. It is DEA's mission to investigate and prosecute drug traffickers and drug trafficking organizations. However, some of the individuals and/or organizations targeted by the DEA may be involved in terrorist activities. In fact, fourteen (or 39 percent) of the State Department's current list of 36 designated foreign terrorist organizations have some degree of connection with drug activities. Due to DEA's global presence and the strong relationship with local law enforcement through the DEA Task Force Program, it is only natural, that in the course of drug investigations and intelligence collection, DEA would develop intelligence and information concerning terrorist organizations.

Defining Narco-Terrorism

According to [U.S. Code] 22 U.S.C. § 2656f(d) (2), terrorism is the premeditated, politically motivated violence against noncombatant targets by sub-national groups or clandestine agents. International terrorism involves citizens, or territory, of more than one country. A terrorist group is any group practicing, or that has significant sub-groups that practice, international terrorism.

Historically, DEA has defined narco-terrorism in terms of Pablo Escobar, the classic cocaine trafficker who used terrorist tactics against noncombatants to further his political agenda and to protect his drug trade. Today, however, governments find themselves faced with classic terrorist groups that participate in, or otherwise receive funds from, drug trafficking to further their agenda. Consequently, law enforcement may seek to distinguish whether narco-terrorists are actual drug traffickers who use terrorism against civilians to advance their agenda, or principally terrorists who out of convenience or necessity, use drug money to further their cause. Our analysis suggests that the label of narco-terrorist may be equally applicable to both groups.

International Efforts to Fight Narco-Terrorism

In central Asia, terrorist insurgents are either funded by the local drug trade or are actually narcotics traffickers pretending to be Islamic insurgents. There is significant evidence that this charge may, in fact, be true. Given the geopolitical stakes involved in central Asia and the American desire for influence there, Washington has promised to support Moscow and local governments in working against "terrorism." One example was the August 2000 meeting of Vyacheslav Trubnikov, first deputy foreign minister of foreign affairs in Russia and former head of Russian intelligence, and Undersecretary of State Thomas Pickering, which led to American statements against terrorism and an agreement between the FBI and Russia's Ministry of Interior to establish a group that will coordinate measures against organized crime.

Such international cooperation, normally involving governmental law-enforcement and intelligence agencies or international organizations like INTERPOL and its European branch EUROPOL, often takes place in contrast to or despite the conflicts among states over issues of defense and political influence—what could be called the traditional or classical security agenda. Thus, even before the Trubnikov-Pickering conversations, Russia and Iran sought more cooperation with U.S. law enforcement against the drug threat despite rivalries on fundamental security issues.

Stephen Blank, *World and I*, December 2001.

DEA defines a narco-terrorist organization as "an organized group that is complicit in the activities of drug trafficking in order to further, or fund, premeditated, politically motivated violence perpetrated against noncombatant targets with the intention to influence (that is, influence a government or group of people).". . .

Narco-Terrorism in South America

One does not have to go to the Middle East to find active terrorist groups—they exist right in our hemisphere. The U.S. State Department has officially designated the National Liberation Army (ELN), the Revolutionary Armed Forces of Colombia (FARC), and the United Self-Defense Groups of Colombia (AUC) as Foreign Terrorist Organizations. These organizations, all based in Colombia, were responsible for some 3,500 murders in 2002. As in years past, Colombia endured more kidnappings [in 2002] than any other country in the world, roughly 3,000. Overall, the AUC, ELN, and FARC all benefit and derive some organizational proceeds from the drug trade, as well as other illegal activities such as kidnapping, extortion, and robbery.

DEA is actively building cases on members of these groups who have been identified as engaging in drug-trafficking related activities, which are summarized below:

March 7, 2002, FARC 16th Front Commander Tomas Molina-Caracas and several of his Colombian and Brazilian criminal associates were indicted in the District of Columbia for conspiring to manufacture and distribute cocaine with the intent and knowledge that it would be illegally imported into the United States. In June 2002, Surinamese authorities detained DEA fugitive Carlos Bolas, a Colombian national and FARC member who was named in the March 2002 indictment. Shortly thereafter, DEA agents transported Bolas from Suriname to the Washington D.C. area for arraignment in U.S. District Court. This marked the first time that the U.S. indicted and arrested a member of a terrorist organization involved in drug trafficking.

On September 24, 2002, the U.S. Government announced an indictment charging leaders of the AUC with trafficking over seventeen tons of cocaine into the United States and Europe beginning in early 1997. Charged in the indictment are AUC leader Carlos Castaño-Gil, AUC military commander Salvatore Mancuso, and AUC member Juan Carlos Sierra-Ramirez. According to the indictment, Carlos Castaño-Gil directed cocaine production and distribution activities in AUC-controlled regions of Colombia.

In November 2002, U.S. Attorney General John Ashcroft announced the takedown of Operation White Terror with the arrests of Fernando Blanco-Puerta, Elkin Arroyave-Ruiz, Uwe Jensen, and Carlos Ali Romero-Varela for their involvement in a multi-million dollar cocaine-for-arms deal. Fernando Blanco-Puerta and Elkin Arroyave-Ruiz were allegedly AUC commanders. All four defendants are charged with conspiracy to distribute cocaine and conspiracy to provide material support and resources to a foreign terrorist organization. This Operation was an Organized Crime Drug Enforcement Task Force (OCDETF) investigation conducted by the Houston offices of the Federal Bureau of Investigation and DEA.

On November 13, 2002, the U.S. Government announced that Jorge Briceño-Suarez was named in a superseding indictment for his narcotics trafficking activities. Jorge Briceño-Suarez commands the Eastern Bloc of the FARC and is a member of the FARC Secretariat. As Eastern Bloc Commander, Briceño-Suarez (direct superior of Tomas Molina-Caracas) is responsible for the activities of four FARC Mini-Blocs that operate in the vast eastern plains of Colombia.

Colombian Terrorism

Revolutionary Armed Forces of Colombia

The FARC, the largest of Colombia's terrorist organizations, uses its relationships with international smuggling organizations to purchase weapons and other equipment on the international black market to be used in the FARC's war against the Colombian government. In some cases, the FARC directly trades cocaine for weapons and in other instances funds weapons purchased with cash derived from cocaine sales.

The FARC are by far the most visibly violent of Colombia's terrorist organizations and have repeatedly demonstrated their willingness to utilize violence to further their agenda. The FARC intensified its terrorist offensive throughout 2002 and 2003 and steadily moved its attacks from the countryside to the cities:

On August 7, 2002, Colombian President Alvaro Uribe was inaugurated amid a FARC mortar attack on the Presidential Palace in the heart of Bogota. One errant mortar killed 21 residents of an impoverished Bogota neighborhood.

On February 7, 2003, a car bomb exploded at Club El Nogal, a popular social club on the north side of Bogota near many residences of U.S. Embassy personnel. Thirty-five persons were killed including several children. The investigation by Colombian authorities revealed that the FARC was responsible for this terrorist act.

On May 5, 2003, Antioquia Governor Guillermo Gaviria and

Gilberto Echeverri, former defense minister and peace adviser, were assassinated by the FARC near Urrao Municipality, Antioquia Department. The two officials were murdered along with eight non-commissioned officers and soldiers.

On May 8, 2003, twenty-eight occupants of a Satena Airline aircraft were terrorized, but otherwise unharmed, when FARC members shot at the aircraft as it was getting ready to land on the runway in La Macarena, Meta (formerly part of the demilitarized zone).

United Self Defense Forces of Colombia and the National Liberation Army

The AUC, commonly referred to as autodefensas or paramilitaries, is an umbrella organization of approximately 13 self-defense groups. The AUC is supported by economic elites (cattle ranchers, emerald miners, coffee plantation owners), drug traffickers, and local communities lacking effective government security, and claims as its primary objective the protection of sponsors from insurgent attacks. The AUC now asserts itself as a regional and national counter-insurgent force. It is adequately equipped and armed, and reportedly pays its members a monthly salary. In 2000, AUC leader Carlos Castano claimed 70 percent of the AUC's operational costs were financed with drug-related earnings, with the balance coming from sponsor donations.

AUC operations vary from assassinating suspected insurgent supporters to engaging guerrilla combat units. Colombian National Police reported the AUC conducted 804 assassinations, 203 kidnappings, and 75 massacres with 507 victims during the first 10 months of 2000. The AUC claims the victims were guerrillas or sympathizers. Combat tactics consist of conventional and guerrilla operations against main force insurgent units. AUC clashes with military and police units are increasing, although the group has traditionally avoided confrontation with government security forces. The paramilitaries have not yet taken action against US personnel.

The ELN—like the FARC—continues to pursue its favored terrorist methods of kidnapping and infrastructure bombing. There are currently no formal or informal peace talks between the ELN and the Colombian government. On March 5, 2003, a car bomb exploded in a shopping center in the northeastern city of Cucuta, killing seven people and injuring more than 50. Military and police sources attributed the Cucuta attack to ELN guerrillas operating in the city.

Terrorism in Mexico and Central America

DEA reporting indicates that persons affiliated with the AUC, and to a lesser extent the FARC, are working with Mexican and Central American trafficking organizations to facilitate cocaine transshipments through the region. Consistent with these reports, a Government of Mexico official recently stated that members of the AUC and the FARC are carrying out drug-trafficking activities in Mexico. There have been numerous instances of drugs-for-weapons exchanges occurring in the region, particularly in Central America, that are exemplified by the November 2002 takedown of Operation White Terror which resulted in the dismantling of an international arms and drug trafficking network linked to the AUC. DEA continues to work with Host Nation Counterparts in Latin America to pursue and disrupt the drug trafficking activities of these vast traditional criminal networks providing financial support to the AUC and the FARC.

Panama

July 22, 2002—After arrests involving the seizure of 10 kilograms of heroin, intelligence revealed that additional drugs were to be located at the beach house of one of the arrested. The police returned to the beach house to find an additional 6 kilograms of heroin, 300 kilograms of cocaine, and 260 kilograms of marijuana. Also discovered were 139 AK-47s, 11 Dragonov sniper rifles 1 Fal 7.62 rifle, 2 .45 caliber submachine guns, 247 AK-47 ammunition clips and 598 rounds of 7.62 bullets.

November 6, 2002—After establishing surveillance at a location where a number of seizures had recently been made, local authorities observed several men carrying large burlap bags. A fire fight occurred after the police approached the men. The police captured one suspect while several others escaped. Subsequently, six additional suspects were apprehended by means of road blocks. The abandoned bags contained 316 kilograms of cocaine, 57 packets of heroin, 410 heroin pellets, and 1,134 small cylinders containing heroin. The next day the police found a cache of AK-47 rifles and other assorted small arms and ammunition in an abandoned pick-up truck that one of the suspects had rented. This seizure like several others in Panama suggest that significant drug transaction orchestrated by Colombian paramilitary groups are often simultaneously accompanied by a significant arms shipment.

DEA intelligence indicates that due to the political and economic crisis in Venezuela, the FARC and AUC are increasingly utilizing Venezuela as a transit zone to smuggle drugs, arms, chemicals and monies to and from Colombia. The declining economy and inability by the Government of Venezuela (GOV) to effectively control the VZ/CB border has resulted in increased drug trafficking, kidnapping and corruption within in the region as a whole. Reporting indicates that some of this activity is directly attributed to the FARC and AUC, as well as other criminal organizations based within the region.

Ecuadorian security forces have worked to reduce the smuggling of arms destined for Colombian terrorist groups and have limited travel at a key border crossing to daytime hours. Nevertheless, armed violence on the Colombian side of the border has contributed to increased lawlessness in Ecuador's northern provinces. . . .

The attacks carried out on our nation on September 11, 2001 graphically illustrated the need to starve the financial base of every terrorist organization and deprive them of drug revenue that is used to fund acts of terror. Narco-terrorist organizations in Colombia and other areas of the world generate millions of dollars in narcotics-related revenues to facilitate their terrorist activities. Tracking and intercepting the unlawful flow of drug money is an important tool in identifying and dismantling international drug trafficking organizations with ties to terrorism. . . .

The events of September 11th have brought new focus to an old problem, narco-terrorism. These events have forever changed the world and demonstrate even the most powerful nation is vulnerable to acts of terrorism. In attempting to combat this threat, the link between drugs and terrorism came to the fore. Whether it is a state, such as formerly Taliban-controlled Afghanistan, or a narco-terrorist organization, such as the FARC, the nexus between drugs and terrorism is perilously evident.

Periodical Bibliography

The following articles have been selected to supplement the diverse views presented in this chapter.

Joe Allen	"Hypocrisy and Terror," *International Socialist Review*, January/February 2002.
William J. Broad, Stephen Engelberg, and James Glanz	"Assessing Risks, Chemical, Biological, Even Nuclear," *New York Times*, November 1, 2001.
Michael Catanzaro	"South America's Drug-Terror Link," *American Enterprise*, June 2002.
Katherine Eban	"Waiting for Bioterror," *Nation*, December 9, 2002.
Ezekiel J. Emanuel	"Chill Out. Anthrax Isn't That Risky," *Wall Street Journal*, October 22, 2001.
Barton Gellman	"Assessing the Smallpox Threat," *Washington Post National Weekly Edition*, November 11–17, 2002.
Jeffrey Goldberg	"In the Party of God," *New Yorker*, October 28, 2002.
Jesse Helms	"Emerging Threats to United States National Security," *Imprimis*, January 2002.
Adrian Karatnycky	"Under Our Very Noses: The Terrorist Next Door," *National Review*, November 5, 2001.
Timothy W. Maier	"Bin Laden Is Not Sole Mastermind," *Insight on the News*, October 29, 2001.
Johanna McGeary	"The New Realities of Terror," *Time*, December 9, 2002.
New Statesman	"Terrorism Thrives When We Turn a Deaf Ear," October 21, 2002.
Dick Ward	"Reassessing Terrorism," *Crime & Justice International*, October/November 2001.
Emily Wax	"An Easy Mark for Terrorism," *Washington Post National Weekly Edition*, December 9–15, 2002.
Fred Weir	"Chechen Women Join Terror's Ranks," *Christian Science Monitor*, June 12, 2003.

What Are the Causes of Terrorism?

Chapter Preface

The September 11, 2001, terrorist attacks in New York, Pennsylvania, and Washington D.C. led to almost-universal sympathy for the United States. Citizens and leaders around the world expressed their grief over the three thousand lives that had been lost and anger at the terrorists who had destroyed America's sense of security for seemingly no other reason than hatred of the United States. However, people from both ends of the political spectrum have questioned whether America was truly innocent or if its foreign policy helped cause the atrocity.

Left-wing political activist Noam Chomsky has asserted that America's foreign policy has caused rancor in the Arab world, which has fostered terrorism against the United States. Arabs have been particularly upset by America's support of UN sanctions against Iraq. Those sanctions, beginning in 1990 following Iraq's invasion of Kuwait, prevented food and medicine from reaching starving and ill Iraqis, leading to hundreds of thousands of deaths. Chomsky also blames U.S. support for Israel, arguing, "The present 'campaign of hatred' in the Arab world is, of course, also fuelled by US policies towards Israel-Palestine. . . . The US has provided the crucial support for Israel's harsh military occupation, now in its 35th year." Such support angers the majority of Arabs, who believe that Israel, widely viewed as a terrorist state, should return its occupied territories to the Palestinians. Chomsky concludes that the United States could reduce the possibility of terrorism by making its foreign policy less inimical to Arabs.

This criticism of U.S. foreign policy is not limited to left-wing commentators nor to discussions about the Middle East. William Norman Grigg, a senior editor for the *New American*, contends that U.S. support of the governments in Bosnia and Kosovo helped provide havens for terrorist leader Osama bin Laden's Muslim terrorist network, al-Qaeda (the group behind the September 11 tragedy). The United States supported Bosnia when the mostly Muslim country declared its independence from Yugoslavia in 1992, resulting in a war against Bosnian Serbs, who opposed inde-

pendence. According to Grigg, U.S. support of the Musl.
government in Bosnia, via American efforts to transport Ira
nian arms to the Bosnian capital, Sarajevo, led to the rise of
Iranian terrorist groups in the war-torn nation—groups that
were allied with bin Laden. Grigg also claims that the
Kosovo Liberation Army, a national police force that the
United States has provided with weapons and training to aid
their efforts to gain Kosovo's independence from Serbia, is
in reality a terrorist group that aids bin Laden and his operatives. Grigg concludes, "What kind of 'war on terrorism'
must we fight when we have found ourselves consistently
lending material, military, and political support to Osama
bin Laden's allies?"

The role U.S. foreign policy played in causing the
September 11 terrorist attacks will probably never be known.
In the following chapter, the authors examine other factors
that lead to terrorism. Whether a result of economics, politics, or religion, terrorism is an exceedingly complex act.

"To pretend that Islam has nothing to do with [September 11] is to willfully ignore the obvious and to forever misinterpret events."

Islam Encourages Terrorism

Ibn Warraq

In the following viewpoint Ibn Warraq asserts that Muslim terrorism has its roots in the Koran, Islam's holy text, and other Islamic writings. According to Ibn Warraq, the Koran is filled with exhortations to fight and kill infidels. He argues that despite the claims of Islam's apologists, jihad is not a defensive measure but instead is defined in Islamic law as an armed struggle against unbelievers, with the ultimate goal being the establishment of a wholly Muslim world. Ibn Warraq asserts that Westerners must recognize that Islam encourages terrorist attacks such as the ones that occurred on September 11, 2001, against the United States. Ibn Warraq is the author of several books, including *Why I Am Not a Muslim* and *The Quest for the Historical Muhammad*. This viewpoint was originally a lecture presented at the twenty-eighth National Convention of American Atheists in Boston on March 30, 2002. Ibn Warraq is a pseudonym, one that dissident authors have traditionally used throughout Islam's history.

As you read, consider the following questions:

1. In Ibn Warraq's view, where is the "totalitarian nature of Islam" most apparent?
2. According to the author, how is Islamic fundamentalism different from any other type of religious fundamentalism?
3. Why does Ibn Warraq believe that moderate Muslims will not declare their love for the United States?

G iven the stupefying enormity of the [the September 11, 2001, terrorist attacks], moral outrage is appropriate and justified, as are demands for punishment. But a civilized society cannot permit blind attacks on all those perceived as "Muslims" or Arabs. Not all Muslims or all Arabs are terrorists. Nor are they implicated in the horrendous events of Tuesday. Police protection for individual Muslims, mosques and other institutions must be increased. However, to pretend that Islam has nothing to do with Terrorist Tuesday is to willfully ignore the obvious and to forever misinterpret events. Without Islam the long-term strategy and individual acts of violence by [terrorist] Usama bin Laden and his followers make little sense. The West needs to understand them in order to be able to deal with them and avoid past mistakes. We are confronted with Islamic terrorists and must take seriously the Islamic component. Westerners in general, and Americans in particular, do not understand the passionate, religious, and anti-western convictions of Islamic terrorists. These God-intoxicated fanatics blindly throw away their lives in return for the Paradise of Seventy Two Virgins offered Muslim martyrs killed in the Holy War against all infidels.

Defining Jihad

[According to the *Dictionary of Islam*] *Jihad* is "a religious war with those who are unbelievers in the mission of the Prophet Muhammad [the Prophet]. It is an incumbent religious duty, established in the Qur'an and in the Traditions as a divine institution, and enjoined specially for the purpose of advancing Islam and repelling evil from Muslims" divided into two spheres: *Dar al-Islam* and *Dar al-Harb*. The latter, the Land of Warfare, is a country belonging to infidels which has not been subdued by Islam. The Dar al-Harb becomes the Dar-al Islam, the Land of Islam, upon the promulgation of the edicts of Islam.

Thus the totalitarian nature of Islam is nowhere more apparent than in the concept of Jihad, the Holy War, whose ultimate aim is to conquer the entire world and subject it to the one true faith, to the law of Allah. To Islam alone has been granted the truth: there is no possibility of salvation outside it.

Muslims must fight and kill in the name of Allah. We read

(IX 5–6): "Kill those who join other gods with God wherever you may find them"; (IV. 76): "Those who believe fight in the cause of God!"; (VIII.39–42): "Say to the Infidels: if they desist from their unbelief, what is now past shall be forgiven; but if they return to it, they have already before them the doom of the ancients! Fight then, against them till strife be at an end, and the religion be all of it God's."

Those who die fighting for the only true religion, Islam, will be amply rewarded in the life to come. (IV.74): "Let those who fight in the cause of God who barter the life of this world for that which is to come; for whoever fights on God's path, whether he is killed or triumphs, We will give him a handsome reward."

Not a Moral Crusade

It is common nowadays for the apologists of Islam, whether Muslims or their Western admirers, to interpret 'Jihad' in the non-military sense of 'moral struggle,' 'moral striving.' But it is quite illegitimate to pretend that the Qur'an and the books on Islamic Law were talking about "moral crusades." Rather as Rudolf Peters says in his definitive study of Jihad, "In the books on Islamic Law, the word means armed struggle against the unbelievers, which is also a common meaning in the Qur'an." Apologists of Islam, even when they do admit that real battles are being referred to, still pretend that the doctrine of Jihad only talks of 'defensive measures,' that is, the apologists pretend that fighting is only allowed to defend Muslims, and that offensive wars are illegitimate. But again, this is not the classical doctrine in Islam; as Peters makes clear, the Sword Verses in the Qur'an were interpreted as unconditional commands to fight the unbelievers, and furthermore these Sword Verses abrogated all previous verses concerning intercourse with non-Muslims. Peters sums up the classical doctrine:

> The doctrine of Jihad as laid down in the works on Islamic Law, developed out of the Koranic prescriptions and the example of the Prophet and the first caliphs, which is recorded in the *hadith*,[1] The crux of the doctrine is the existence of

1. *Hadith* is a narration of Muhammad's life.

one single Islamic state, ruling the entire *umma* [Muslim community].

It is the duty of the *umma* to expand the territory of this state in order to bring as many people under its rule as possible. The ultimate aim is to bring the whole earth under the sway of Islam and to extirpate unbelief: "Fight them until there is no persecution and the religion is God's entirely." (sura ii.193; viii.39). Expansionist jihad is a collective duty (*fard ala al-kifitya*), which is fulfilled if a sufficient number of people take part in it. If this is not the case, the whole *umma* is sinning.

Here are more bellicose verses from the Qur'an, the words of Allah telling Muslims to kill and murder on his behalf:

ii. 193: Fight against them until idolatry is no more and Allah's religion reigns supreme.

ii. 216: Fighting is obligatory for you, much as you dislike it. But you may hate a thing although it is good for you, and love a thing although it is bad for you. Allah knows, but you do not.

ix. 41: Whether unarmed or well-equipped, march on and fight for the cause of Allah, with your wealth and your persons. This is best for you, if you but knew it.

ix. 123: Believers! Make war on the infidels who dwell around you let them find harshness in you.

lxvi. 9: O Prophet! Make war on the unbelievers and the hypocrites and deal sternly with them. Hell shall be their home, evil their fate.

ix. 73: O Prophet! Make war on the unbelievers and the hypocrites. Be harsh with them. Their ultimate abode is hell, a hapless journey's end.

viii. 65: O Prophet! Exhort the believers to fight. If there are twenty steadfast men among you, they shall vanquish two hundred; and if there are a hundred, they shall rout a thousand unbelievers, for they are devoid of understanding.

xlvii. 4–15: When you meet the unbelievers in the battlefield strike off their heads and when you have laid them low, bind your captives firmly. . . .

xxv. 52: Do not yield to the unbelievers, but fight them strenuously with this Qur'an.

Finally, on the obligation of Jihad, I shall quote from two Muslim thinkers greatly admired in the West. First, Ibn Khaldun in his *Muqaddimah* writes: "In the Muslim community, the holy war is religious duty, because of the universalism of the Muslim mission and (the obligation to) convert everybody to Islam either by persuasion or by force."

A Primitive Ideology

Nearly every country in the Middle East is a dictatorship. These countries are wracked with the chronic poverty bred by dictatorship—with the exception of the rulers, who pocket money from oil reserves discovered, drilled, and made valuable by Western capital and technology. All of these countries are overrun—or are on the verge of being overrun—by religious fanatics who ruthlessly suppress any manifestation of the pursuit of happiness in this world, from baring one's ankles to watching television.

The ideology of the enemy is clear. It is a primitive form of religious fundamentalism. It holds as its ideal total immolation in the service of God, as practiced by suicide bombers. It preaches the use of physical force to impose religious strictures, as enforced, in ascending order of brutality, by the religious police of Saudi Arabia, by the government of Iran, and by Afghanistan's religious Gestapo, the Taliban. It is driven by a ruthless religious intolerance, as seen in the Taliban's threat of death sentences against Christian missionaries and Osama bin Laden's holy war to drive the "infidels," Jews and Americans, from the Middle East.

Robert Tracinski, *Intellectual Activist*, November 2001.

And now Averroës, a much romanticized figure in the West: "According to the majority of scholars, the compulsory nature of the jihad is founded on sura ii.216: 'Prescribed for you is fighting, though it is hateful to you.' The obligation to participate in the jihad applies to adult free men who have the means at their disposal to go to war and who are healthy. . . . Scholars agree that all polytheists should be fought; This is founded on sura viii.39: Fight them until there is no persecution and the religion is God's entirely.". . . Most scholars are agreed that in his dealing with captives, various policies are open to the Imam. He may pardon them, enslave them, kill them, or release them either on ransom or as *dhimmi* [non-Muslim, second class subject of the Islamic state], in which latter case the released captive is obliged to pay poll-tax (*jizya*). . . . Sura viii.67 'It is not for any Prophet to have prisoners until he make wide slaughter in the land.'. . . . the occasion when this verse was revealed [*viz.* the captives of Badr] would prove that it is better to kill captives than to enslave them. The Prophet himself would in some cases kill captives outside the field of battle, while he would pardon them in others. Women he used to enslave. . . . The Muslims are agreed that the aim of warfare against the People of the Book . . . is two-fold: either conversion to Islam or payment of poll-tax-*jizya*).". . .

The Qur'an Must Be Examined

It is surely time for us who live in the West and enjoy freedom of expression to examine unflinchingly and unapologetically the tenets of these fanatics, including the Qur'an which divinely sanctions violence. (I may add that we should celebrate our freedoms in the West: Imagine living in Iran where women and men are still being stoned to death for adultery. In this country we get stoned first and *then* commit adultery.)

We should unapologetically examine the life of the Prophet, who was not above political assassinations, and who was responsible for the massacre of the Jews. "Ah, but you are confusing Islam with Islamic fundamentalism. The *real* Islam has nothing to do with violence," apologists of Islam argue.

There may be moderate Muslims, but Islam itself is not moderate. There is no difference between Islam and Islamic fundamentalism: at most there is a difference of degree but not of kind.

There is a well-known saying which asks, What is the difference between a moderate Islamist and a fundamentalist Islamist? The answer is: the moderate is the one who has run out of ammunition. This is obvious for me in today's Afghanistan: all that has changed is the size of the stones used when stoning some adulteress to death. The stones are smaller, prolonging the torture of the victim. Such is Islamic clemency!

All the tenets of Islamic fundamentalism are derived from the Qur'an, the Sunna,[2] and the Hadith—Islamic fundamentalism is a totalitarian construct derived by Muslim jurists from the fundamental and defining texts of Islam. The fundamentalists, with greater logic and coherence than so-called

2. *Sunna* is the way in which Muhammad lived his life.

75

moderate or liberal Muslims, have made Islam the basis of a radical utopian ideology that aims to replace capitalism and democracy as the reigning world system. Islamism accounts for the anti-American hatred to be found in places far from the Arab-Israeli conflict, like Nigeria and Afghanistan, demonstrating that the Middle East conflict cannot legitimately be used to explain this phenomenon called Islamism. A Palestinian involved in the WTC [World Trade Center] bombings would be seen as a martyr to the Palestinian cause, but even more as a martyr to Islam.

"Ah, but Islamic fundamentalism is like any other kind of fundamentalism, one must not demonize it. It is the result of political, social grievances. It must be explained in terms of economics and not religion," continue the apologists of Islam. There are enormous differences between Islamic fundamentalism and any other kind of modern fundamentalism. It is true that Hindu, Jewish, and Christian fundamentalists have been responsible for acts of violence, but these have been confined to particular countries and regions. Islamic fundamentalism has global aspirations: the submission of the entire world to the all-embracing Shari'a, Islamic Law, a fascist system of dictates designed to control every single act of all individuals. Nor do Hindus or Jews seek to convert the world to their religion. Christians do indulge in proselytism but no longer use acts of violence or international terrorism to achieve their aims.

Only Islam treats non-believers as inferior beings who are expendable in the drive to world hegemony. Islam justifies any means to achieve the end of establishing an Islamic world. Islamic fundamentalists recruit among Muslim populations, they appeal to Islamic religious symbols, and they motivate their recruits with Islamic doctrine derived from the Qur'an. . . .

What Moderate Muslims Must Do

Surely it is time for moderate Muslims to stand up and be counted. I should like to see them do three things:

1. All moderate Muslims should unequivocally denounce this barbarism. They should condemn it for what it is: the butchery of innocent people.

2. All moderate Muslim citizens of the United States should proclaim their Americanness, their patriotism, and

their solidarity with the families of the victims. They should show their pride in their country by giving blood and other aid to victims and their families.

3. All moderate Muslims should take this opportunity to examine the tenets of their faith; should look at the Qur'an, recognize its role in the instigation of religious violence, and see it for what it is: a problematical human document reflecting seventh or perhaps eighth-century values which the West has largely outgrown.

While it should not be too difficult for moderate Muslims to accept the need to denounce the violence of Terrorist Tuesday, I am not at all optimistic about their courage or willingness to proclaim their love for their chosen country, the USA, or examine the Qur'an critically.

Too many Muslims are taught from an early age that their first allegiance is to Islam. They are exhorted in sermons in mosques, and in books by such Muslim intellectuals as Dr. [Kalim] Siddiqui of the Muslim Institute in London, that if the laws of the land conflict with any of the tenets of Islam, then they must break the laws of the infidels, and only follow the Law of God, the Shari'a Islamic Law.

It is a remarkable fact that at the time of the Gulf War, a high proportion of Muslims living in the West supported [Iraqi leader] Saddam Hussein. In the aftermath of the WTC terror, it is now clear from reports in the media that many Muslims, even those living in the West, see these acts of barbarism as acts of heroism; they give their unequivocal support to their hero, Usama bin Laden.

Few Muslims have shown themselves capable of scrutinizing their sacred text rationally. Indeed any criticism of their religious tenets is taken as an insult to their faith, for which so many Muslims seem ready to kill—as in the Rushdie affair or the Taslima Nasreen affair.[3] Muslims seem to be unaware that the research of western scholars concerning the existence of figures such as Abraham, Isaac, and Joseph or the authorship of the Pentateuch [the five books of the

3. Salman Rushdie was condemned to death by the Ayatollah Khomeini, Iran's spiritual leader, after Rushdie published the *Satanic Verses*, a book considered heretical by fundamentalist Muslims. Taslima Nasreen is a Bangladeshi writer who received a death threat from Islamic militants following the publication of her book *Shame*, which contained descriptions of Muslims persecuting Hindus.

Torah] applies directly to their belief system.

Furthermore, it is surely totally irrational to continue to believe that the Qur'an is the word of God when the slightest amount of rational thought will reveal that the Qur'an contains words and passages *addressed to God (e.g.* VI.104; VI.114; XLII.1; XXVII.91; LXXXI.15–29; LXXXIV. 16–19; *etc.*); or that it is full of historical errors and inconsistencies.

Respect for other cultures, for other values than our own, is a hallmark of a civilized society. But Multiculturalism is based on some fundamental misconceptions. First, there is the erroneous and sentimental belief that all cultures, deep down, have the same values; or, at least if different, are equally worthy of respect. But the truth is that not all cultures have the same values, and not all values are worthy of respect. There is nothing sacrosanct about customs or cultural traditions: they can change under criticism. After all, the secularist values of the West are not much more than two hundred years old.

If these other values are destructive of our own cherished values, are we not justified in fighting them—both by intellectual means (that is by reason and argument, and criticism) and by legal means (by making sure the laws and constitution of the country are respected by all)? It becomes a duty to defend those values that we would live by. But here western intellectuals have sadly failed in defending western values, such as rationalism, social pluralism, human rights, the rule of law, representative government, individualism (in the sense that every individual counts, and no individual should be sacrificed for some utopian future collective end), freedom of expression, freedom of and from religion, the rights of minorities, and so on.

Instead, the so-called experts on Islam in western universities, in the media, in the churches and even in government bureaus have become apologists for Islam. They bear some responsibility for creating an atmosphere little short of intellectual terrorism where any criticism of Islam is denounced as fascism, racism, or "orientalism." They bear some responsibility for lulling the public into thinking that "The Islamic Threat" is a myth. It is our duty to fight this intellectual terrorism. It is our duty to defend the values of liberal democracy.

| "Terrorism is not only un-Islamic but anti-Islamic, and those who commit terrorism should be designated as criminals rather than as holy warriors."

Islam Does Not Encourage Terrorism

Antony T. Sullivan

In the following viewpoint Antony T. Sullivan contends that Islam does not condone terrorism. He argues that terrorism is an "unholy war," or *hiraba*, an act that has been repeatedly castigated in the Islamic holy book, the Koran, and scholarly texts. According to Sullivan, Westerners and many Muslims are wrong to equate terrorism with jihad, which should instead be understood as a largely nonmilitary effort to create a better world. Sullivan concludes that Muslims who wish to reclaim their faith from the extremists who are deforming it through acts of terrorism must make it clear that both the words of the Koran and the idea of jihad call for peace and not violence. Sullivan is an associate at the Center for Middle Eastern and North African Studies at the University of Michigan and a member of the board of directors of the Center for the Study of Islam and Democracy.

As you read, consider the following questions:
1. In Sullivan's opinion, what good news emerged in the aftermath of the September 11, 2001, terrorist attacks?
2. According to Professor Sherman A. Jackson, how have Muslims traditionally understood *hiraba*?
3. How should wars be fought when they are unavoidable, according to the author?

Antony T. Sullivan, "New Frontiers in the Ecumenical Jihad Against Terrorism: Terrorism, Jihad, and the Struggle for New Understandings," *American Muslim*, January/February 2003. Copyright © 2003 by *American Muslim*. Reproduced by permission.

These are difficult times in relations between the West and the Islamic world. Wars and rumors of war abound, and terrorism (although rarely its context) dominates the headlines. A shooting war continues between the United States and [terrorist organization] al Qaa'ida in Afghanistan, and war evidently impends between the United States and the United Kingdom on the one hand and Iraq on the other.[1]

Fundamentalisms—Muslim, Jewish, and Christian—metastasize. Atop all else, violence reigns unchecked in Israel and the Occupied Territories, and makes effective responses to assorted other challenges enormously more difficult. With polarities unprecedented in modern times between the West and the Islamic world, and seething anger among Muslims worldwide against the United States, it is difficult indeed to discuss objectively concepts with such emotive resonance as terrorism and Jihad. But the attempt to do so has never been more important.

Terrorism Is Not Jihad

It is unfortunate that in the West a putative validation of terrorism has come to be understood as incarnated in the Arabic word Jihad. And in the Islamic world, far too many today understand Jihad as justifying, indeed demanding, the taking of the lives of innocent civilians in countries or cultures against which Arabs and Muslims may have very real and painful grievances. Misperceptions, and rampant ignorance, reign almost everywhere. Especially in the United States and the Arab world, there is today an enormous need for an intellectual and spiritual "Jihad," or effort, to readdress soberly the whole issue of terrorism, and the significance of the concept of Jihad over the entire span of Islamic history.

My fundamental argument is that terrorism and Jihad are not identical twins but historic enemies. I will maintain that a new vocabulary is essential to demonstrate the radical antipathy that has separated these concepts until very recent decades. Terrorism is not only un-Islamic but anti-Islamic, and those who commit terrorism should be designated as criminals rather

1. In fall 2001, the United States went to war in Afghanistan to topple its government, which had supported the terrorist group responsible for the September 11 attacks. A war in Iraq occurred in spring 2003, with the goal of overthrowing dictator Saddam Hussein.

than as holy warriors or resistance fighters. . . .

If the perceived linkage between terrorism and Jihad can be ruptured, and Jihad reconceptualized as constituting a means by which all of the children of Abraham may strive to create a better world, the foundations for a brighter future will surely have been laid. . . .

The fact is that apprehension of terrorism may be similar to apprehension of pornography. Namely, and like pornography, terrorism may be difficult to define in a fashion that wins universal approbation, but we all surely recognize it, as we do pornography, when we see it. No one—anywhere—should infuse terrorism with any sort of religious rationale or justification. Terrorism constitutes criminal behavior, and specific designation of terrorism as criminal cannot be said too loudly, or too frequently, by the most prominent representatives of Islam, Christianity, and Judaism. Terrorist criminality can be and is indeed being practiced today by states as well as by individuals and groups, and one should never hesitate to make this clear. In the aftermath of [the September 11, 2001, terrorist attacks] the good news is that prominent Muslims have time and again uttered condemnations of terrorism committed by Arabs and/or Muslims. The bad news is that these condemnations have failed to penetrate the consciousness of most Americans, and most assuredly have not influenced the formulation of U.S. foreign policy in Washington, D.C.

I believe that the title of this particular panel ("Conceptualizing Jihad and Terrorism")[2] may have the unintended consequence of projecting exactly the sort of "linkage" between the two terms that the conference organizers undoubtedly wish to avoid. What is now needed, I believe, is a new and authentically Islamic vocabulary that definitively separates the concept of Jihad from that of terrorism. Some of that Islamic vocabulary already exists, and it is time for ever more Muslims to begin to use it, I would argue, when engaged in discussion of this topic. Other vocabulary perhaps needs to be resuscitated, and applied in novel ways. Ijtihad, or interpretation, of the Quran, hadith, and fiqh[3]

2. The January/February 2003 issue of *American Muslim* featured several articles on that topic.   3. The Quran (Koran) is Islam's holy book; hadith is a narration of the prophet Muhammad's life; and fiqh is Islamic jurisprudence.

should today be considered not only permissible, but obligatory, for all Muslims.

Terrorism Is an Unholy War

The venerable Islamic concept of Hiraba is one such ancient term that merits greatly renewed emphasis now. It is that word, designating "unholy war" and derived from the Arabic root hariba meaning to be "furious" or "enraged," that Muslims need to begin to employ, I believe, when discussing the phenomenon of terrorism. Specifically, I propose that anything that is clearly terrorism be described as Hiraba, not Jihad. Indeed, I believe that Jihad should today largely be restricted to describe non-military endeavors, and used especially in the context of the traditional Islamic understanding of the "Greater Jihad."[4] In addition, of course, Jihad should continue to be used to denote what is clearly defensive warfare: but the fact that such warfare is defensive only, and why, needs to be clearly explained. In that particular regard, one can do no better than to begin with the Quranic verse: "To those against whom war is made, permission is given (to fight), because they are wronged . . ." (22:39). The key concepts here, of course, are the "wrong" done to the believers by others who initiate war against them, and the consequent obligation of Muslims to respond in kind to protect their faith and community.

The Quran is emphatic and categorical in its condemnation of Hiraba. Thus: "[Verily] the punishment of those who wage war (yuhariboona) against God and his Messenger, and strive with might and main for mischief through the land, is: execution, or crucifixion, or the cutting off of hands and feet from opposite sides, or exile from the land: That is their disgrace in this world, and a heavy punishment is theirs in the hereafter" (5: 33). The classical medieval Arab commentators explained what they understood this Quranic condemnation of Hiraba to mean. For example, the Spanish Maliki jurist Ibn Abd al-Barr defines the committer of Hiraba as "Anyone who disturbs free passage in the streets and renders them unsafe to travel, striving to spread corruption through the land

4. a spiritual war against the devil and one's sins

by taking money, killing people or violating what God has made it unlawful to violate, is guilty of Hiraba . . ." Imam al-Narwawi states that "Whoever brandishes a weapon and terrorizes the streets . . . must be pursued by the authorities because if he is left unmolested his power will increase . . . and corruption will spread." And Ibn Qudamah defines Hiraba as "the act of openly holding people up. . .with weapons to take their money." What is common to all of these definitions, as Professor Sherman A. Jackson has pointed out, is that Hiraba has traditionally been understood by Muslims to mean the attempt to intimidate an entire civilian population, and the effort to spread a sense of fear and helplessness as widely as possible in society. Could one ask for better designations of what we today call terrorism? And is it not precisely the realization of such social paralysis that contemporary groups like al-Qaa'ida are attempting to accomplish?

Morin. © 2001 by Jim Morin. Reproduced by permission of King Features Syndicate.

In traditional Islamic parlance, Hiraba clearly means not only "unholy war," but also "warfare against society." As defined by Professor Khalid Abou 'al Fadl, it means "killing by stealth and targeting a defenseless victim in a way intended to cause terror in society." The concept of Hiraba is closely 'connected with that of "fitna," which designates the disruption of established political and social order. Fitna, like Hiraba, was long considered by Islamic jurists to be among the crimes meriting the most severe of punishments. When Muslims refer to the activities of organizations allied with or sympathetic to [terrorist] Usama bin Laden and al Qaa'ida—many of which use the word Jihad to describe themselves and their activities but are so evidently engaged in fitna—they would do well to begin to describe such organizations as irhabi (terrorist) rather than jihadi.

Moreover, there are assorted terms in traditional Islamic vocabulary in addition to Hiraba that also may deserve revival. Those terms include mufsidun, tajdif, and shaitaniyya. The challenge for all those who wish to reclaim Islam from those who currently are deforming it, and thereby to begin to educate the West concerning the true nature of Islamic revelation, is first and foremost to launch a "Jihad" to reclaim the vocabulary of violence from those extremists who are now so blackening the reputation of Islam by their frequently unchallenged use of the words they do.

Of all allied understandings, the Islamic concept of "tajdif" has long been intimately associated with Hiraba. Tajdif designates the blasphemy that results from the waging of unholy warfare by evildoers. Tajdif has traditionally been considered by Muslims as an act of apostasy punishable by death. The term "mufsidun" designates those who engage in Hiraba, and who perpetrate what we today understand as terrorism. Tajdif, and the activities of mufsidun, have traditionally been understood by Muslims as examples of shaitaniyya, or Satanic and anti-Islamic activity. Today, the fact is that increasing numbers of Muslim scholars and students of Islam, both in the West and the Islamic world, are beginning to use the vocabulary associated with Hiraba and are urging others to do the same. To the extent that Hiraba can come to replace Jihad, in Jihad's deformed and un-Islamic sense, the better off, I would argue, all of us will be. . . .

Choosing Peace over War

Throughout the Quran, the concept of Jihad is employed not to sanctify unbridled violence but to facilitate the realization of a political and social order in which peace might prevail. Even when war was imposed on the Muslim community, believers are counseled "not [to] transgress limits; for God loveth not [such] transgressors" (2:190). In other words, war when unavoidable should be fought in a fashion to enhance the possibilities for peace, rather than in any way that might make the subsequent realization of peace difficult or impossible. Perhaps most famously, the Quran commands Muslims to accept peace even in the middle of hostilities if the enemy suddenly indicates a desire for it. Thus: "But if the enemy incline towards peace, do you (also) incline towards peace, and trust in God: for He is the One that heareth and knoweth (all things). Should they [the enemy] intend to deceive you—verily God is sufficient to you: He it is that has strengthened you with His aid and with (the company of) the Believers" (8:61, 62). Today, when some have so badly confused Jihad with terrorism, and have forgotten that Jihad is the antithesis of Hiraba, a rereading of the Quran would seem to be very much in order.

"Economic democracy and economic sovereignty are preconditions for peace and security. Globalization destroys both, while fueling terrorism and violence."

Economic Problems Cause Terrorism

Vandana Shiva

Many political analysts have suggested that terrorism could be reduced in impoverished nations if the West provided economic assistance to them. However, not everyone believes that terrorism is caused by economic backwardness. In fact, the economic problems stemming from globalization—inequitable resource appropriation, the destruction of small farms, and the growing power of corporations—is a major cause of terrorism, Vandana Shiva asserts in the following viewpoint. In Shiva's view, claims that globalization leads to diversity and democracy and that terrorists originate primarily from nonglobalized countries are misguided. Shiva argues that the entrance of global corporations into developing nations instead leads to economic insecurity, as local jobs are destroyed: this insecurity breeds fundamentalism, fear, and ultimately terrorism and violence. Shiva is an ecologist, artist, and the director of the Research Foundation for Science, Technology, and Natural Resource Policy, an organization that researches sustainable agriculture and development.

As you read, consider the following questions:

1. Why does Shiva believe globalization should not be equated with open societies?
2. What do open global markets create, according to Shiva?

Vandana Shiva, "Open Markets, Closed Minds," *Toward Freedom*, vol. 51, Winter 2003, p. 3. Copyright © 2003 by Vandana Shiva. Reproduced by permission.

[In September 2002] in a *New York Times* column titled, "Globalization, Alive and Well" Thomas Friedman falsely claimed that the gifts of pluralism, diversity, democracy, which societies like India have evolved over millennia, are the result of currently practiced corporate globalization. Thus, he transforms into intrinsic perversions the violence and exclusions that result from imperialism and undemocratic, ruthless, irresponsible, economic globalization, trade liberalization, and resource appropriation. Offering a flawed and misplaced analysis on the roots of terrorism, he also argues that globalization is an antidote to terrorism.

Rising Political and Social Tensions

In reality, among the consequences of the insecurity and polarization created by both [the September 11, 2001, terrorist attacks] and globalization are the increased communalization of politics in India, as well as heightened tensions between India and Pakistan. Even Gujarat, the land of Gandhi, has been transformed into a hotbed of violence. Thousands of Muslims have died in communal violence in Gujarat, the Indian state most integrated into the global economy. The killers were economically globalized but culturally parochial. They drove fancy cars and had mobile phones, and their targets were Muslim business establishments.

As the genocide in Gujarat makes clear, economic integration and economic "openness" on terms that generate inequality and insecurity can go hand in hand with social disintegration and economic and political "closure" and exclusion. In fact, undemocratic, unequitable, unjust integration through global markets is precisely what fuels fundamentalism, intolerance, xenophobia, and violence across the world.

Equating globalization with open societies is inaccurate and intellectually sloppy. Economic "openness" for multinational corporations (MNCs), under the rules of corporate globalization, means "economic closure" for domestic producers. For example, India's small-scale industry is closing down, destroying millions of jobs. Open markets for agribusiness like Cargill means market closure for Indian farmers, whose markets and incomes are destroyed by dumping and the removal of import restrictions (known as "Quantitative Restrictions," or QRs in WTO [World Trade Organization] jargon). Market openness for Monsanto's costly hybrid and genetically modified (GM) seeds means economic closure for indebted farmers who are committing suicide, and market closure for small-scale organic producers whose crops get contaminated by the genetically engineered seeds. For the large majority in India, globalization has created new poverty and destitution.

Not only does market "openness" for global corporations not translate into openness for domestic economies, the destruction of jobs, livelihoods and economic security creates inflammable societies that become vulnerable to terrorism and fundamentalism. Terrorism is a child of exclusion and insecurity. Both are unavoidable outcomes of globalization.

Isolation Is Not to Blame

According to Friedman, "If one thing stands out from 9/11, it's the fact that the terrorists originated from the least globalized, least open, least integrated corners of the world, namely Saudi Arabia, Yemen, Afghanistan, and Northwest Pakistan. Countries that don't trade in goods and services also tend not to trade in ideas, pluralism and tolerance."

He is wrong at every level of his argument. First, Saudi Arabia is totally integrated into the global economy. Its oil props up the US economy. Oil is at the heart of US military presence in Saudi Arabia, and the US military presence in defense of oil interests is at the root of the transformation of Osama Bin Laden into a terrorist. Global terrorism emerged from the global oil economy and global militarism.

The violence in Afghanistan and the rise of terrorism did not emerge because that nation was isolated from the world. Rather, it became the ground for global conflict and superpower rivalry over control of central Asian oil. Afghanistan is an ancient trading nation. Long before the US was born, Afghans were trading throughout Asia. As children we bought dried fruits from traders who came from Kabul and sold goods door to door. A lovely film, *Kabuliwala*, which I saw many times, was based on the beautiful relationship between a Kabul trader and a little Indian girl.

Creating Fundamentalism

Whether it is Afghanistan or Gujarat in India, globalization is destroying the fabric of pluralism and tolerance. As resources are snatched by global corporations, as livelihoods and jobs are destroyed to transform our economies into markets for products from MNCs, economic insecurity is created. This insecurity becomes fertile ground for fundamentalism, hatred, fear, and intolerance.

Fundamentalism becomes the dominant characteristic of politics as economic sovereignty and democracy are eroded by globalization, which shifts economic decisions from people's lives and national democracies to undemocratic institutions like the WTO, World Bank and IMF [International Monetary Fund], and corporations whose only objective is profits. Global market integration is creating social and political exclusion, and "open markets" are creating "closed minds."

Attacks on American Culture

The U.S. commercial and cultural presence overseas—although it cannot be linked as directly to U.S. policies as diplomatic or military installations can—has been the target of terrorism conducted solely for reasons of symbolism and hatred (as distinct from more instrumental uses of terrorism such as hostage taking, in which U.S. business has also figured as a target). Leftists, for example, have frequently struck U.S.-owned business as blows against "economic imperialism." Attacks by Greek leftists in 1999 alone included hits against offices of American Express and Chase Manhattan, a General Motors dealership, and a McDonald's. . . .

The leftists have opposed this America violently because to them it is the font of economic exploitation. The Islamists oppose it violently because to them it is the font of a torrent of dirty water that is polluting the pond where they live.

Paul R. Pillar, *Terrorism and U.S. Foreign Policy*, 2001.

Open minds are products of stable and secure conditions in society. But open global markets do not create open minds; rather, they create massive political and economic instability.

Globalization is a political and economic hurricane. When

Gandhi led India's freedom movement on the principles of Swadeshi[1] and economic sovereignty, he was accused of being an isolationist. In response, he said, "I want the winds of all cultures to blow freely through my doors and windows. But I do not want any storm to blow away my house."

Cultural openness comes through the doors and windows we open when societies choose the terms of integration. Cultural and political closure and shut down is the inevitable outcome of destructive, coercive, undemocratic market integration over which societies have no control.

India's Legacies

Friedman has cited Jairam Ramesh of India's Congress Party as a supporter of globalization. Yet two Congress chief ministers have been arrested for protesting trade liberalization policies, especially in agriculture. Why? Because globalization has eroded farm incomes, pushing prices below the cost of production and destroying rural livelihoods. In fact, the ruling party is split on globalization, with three ministers blocking privatization of the public sector. In India, globalization is hotly contested and often blocked. Its main legacy is social and political unrest and instability.

Friedman also has a habit of claiming as gifts of globalization the legacies of pluralism and democracy that our societies have built over millennia, and that it actually threatens. He perversely assigns to non-western societies the social, cultural, economic destruction caused by Western colonization.

Even our scientific and technological strength, which Friedman attributes to globalization, is a legacy of centuries of Indian mathematical genius, and more recent experience in scientific and technological self-reliance. Bangalore is the Silicon Valley of India because Sri C.V. Raman, a Nobel Laureate in Physics, built institutes of excellence, and because indigenous businesses financed them. For half a century, India has built public sector institutions like Bharat Electronics, National Aeronautical Labs, and Hindustan Ma-

1. Swadeshi was an economic movement, supported by Gandhi, that aimed to increase employment by encouraging village industries that do not rely on deadly machinery and chemicals.

chine Tools. Bangalore's science and technology capacity was built through policies of self-reliance, not globalization. The benefits came from policies of self-determination, nation building, and public investment in public goods.

India's Silicon Valley, as well as the US version, benefited from this indigenous technological capacity building. Indians from lower middle-class and rural backgrounds have obtained technical training because of India's educational policies. The country's technological capacities are a product of treating higher education as a public good, not a privatized marketable service. In fact, it is precisely because India's education and research systems were accessible as public services that so many young people from less privileged backgrounds could get technically trained. This is a result of India's public investment in education, not globalization.

Sowing Destructive Seeds

In fact, as education is privatized and globalized, less privileged youth are being denied access. It is precisely this denial and exclusion from education and jobs which makes them prey to fundamentalist right-wing forces. Under World Bank Structural Adjustment programs, our educational systems are being dismantled. Universities can't run labs and libraries. As education and research is further privatized through the WTO'S General Agreement on Trade in Services (GATS), our youth will be further denied rights to education that previous generations could take for granted in a free and independent, pre-globalization India.

Globalization is rupturing that delicate fabric of equity, democracy, and pluralism. At the same time, it is sowing the seeds of inequality, exclusion, fundamentalism, and violence. Economic democracy and economic sovereignty are preconditions for peace and security. Globalization destroys both, while fueling terrorism and violence. Thus, it carries the seeds of its own destruction.

Fortunately, Friedman's false and unreliable analysis of cultures and societies he neither knows nor understands cannot rescue this failed project. Kept alive by lies and military force, its ultimate destination is the dustbin of history.

| *"Militant Islam (or Islamism) is not a response to poverty or impoverishment."*

Economic Problems Do Not Cause Terrorism

Daniel Pipes

Many scholars have argued that poverty is a root cause of terrorism and that by providing economic assistance to developing nations, Western countries can reduce the spread of terror. In the following viewpoint Daniel Pipes disputes this claim by contending that economic distress does not lead to terrorism. According to Pipes, militant Muslims—including Palestinian suicide bombers and the September 11, 2001, hijackers—are more likely to be educated and well employed. In fact, Pipes concludes, impoverished Muslims are more likely to turn away from fundamentalism during politically and economically difficult times. Pipes is the director of the Middle East Forum and the author of several books, including *The Hidden Hand: Middle East Fears of Conspiracy* and *The Long Shadow: Culture and Politics in the Middle East.*

As you read, consider the following questions:
1. What is an "Islamic economy," as quoted by Pipes?
2. How does the author describe a typical member of a militant Islamic party?
3. Why does Pipes conclude that Westernization does not provide a solution to militant Islam?

The events of September 11, 2001, have intensified a long-standing debate: What causes Muslims to turn to militant Islam? Some analysts have noted the poverty of Afghanistan[1] and concluded that herein lay the problem. Jessica Stern of Harvard University wrote that the United States "can no longer afford to allow states to fail." If it does not devote a much higher priority to health, education and economic development abroad, she writes, "new Osamas will continue to arise." Susan Sachs of the *New York Times* observes: "Predictably, the disappointed youth of Egypt and Saudi Arabia turn to religion for comfort." More colorfully, others have advocated bombarding Afghanistan with foodstuffs not along with but instead of explosives.

Behind these analyses lies an assumption that socioeconomic distress drives Muslims to extremism. The evidence, however, does not support this expectation. Militant Islam (or Islamism) is not a response to poverty or impoverishment; not only are Bangladesh and Iraq not hotbeds of militant Islam, but militant Islam has often surged in countries experiencing rapid economic growth. The factors that cause militant Islam to decline or flourish appear to have more to do with issues of identity than with economics.

A Widely Held Belief

The conventional wisdom—that economic stress causes militant Islam and that economic growth is needed to blunt it—has many well-placed adherents. Even some Islamists themselves accept this connection. In the words of a fiery sheikh from Cairo, "Islam is the religion of bad times." A Hamas [terrorist] leader in Gaza, Mahmud az-Zahar, says, "It is enough to see the poverty-stricken outskirts of Algiers or the refugee camps in Gaza to understand the factors that nurture the strength of the Islamic Resistance Movement." In this spirit, militant Islamic organizations offer a wide range of welfare benefits in an effort to attract followers. They also promote what they call an "Islamic economy" as the "most gracious system of solidarity in a society. Under such a system,

1. Afghanistan's former government, the Islamic fundamentalist Taliban, helped fund the terrorists behind the September 11 attacks. Osama bin Laden was the leader responsible for the attacks.

the honorable do not fall, the honest do not perish, the needy do not suffer, the handicapped do not despair, the sick do not die for lack of care, and people do not destroy one another."

Many secular Muslims also stress militant Islam's source in poverty as an article of faith. Süleyman Demirel, the former Turkish president, says, "As long as there is poverty, inequality, injustice, and repressive political systems, fundamentalist tendencies will grow in the world." Turkey's former prime minister, Tansu Ciller, finds that Islamists did so well in the 1994 elections because "People reacted to the economy." The chief of Jordanian Army Intelligence holds, "Economic development may solve almost all of our problems [in the Middle East]." Including militant Islam, he was asked? Yes, he replied: "The moment a person is in a good economic position, has a job, and can support his family, all other problems vanish."

Leftists in the Middle East concur, interpreting the militant Islamic resurgence as "a sign of pessimism. Because people are desperate, they are resorting to the supernatural." Social scientists sign on as well: Hooshang Amirahmadi, an academic of Iranian origins, argues that "the roots of Islamic radicalism must be looked for outside the religion, in the real world of cultural despair, economic decline, political oppression, and spiritual turmoil in which most Muslims find themselves today." The academy, with its lingering Marxist disposition and disdain for faith, of course accepts this militant Islam-from-poverty thesis with near unanimity. [History professor] Ervand Abrahamian holds that "the behavior of [Iranian cleric and leader Ayatollah Ruhollah] Khomeini and the Islamic Republic has been determined less by scriptural principles than by immediate political, social and economic needs." Ziad Abu-Amr, author of a book on militant Islam (and a member of the Palestine Legislative Council), ascribes a Palestinian turn toward religiosity to "the sombre climate of destruction, war, unemployment, and depression [which] cause people to seek solace, and they're going to Allah."

The Western Interpretation

Western politicians also find the argument compelling. For former President Bill Clinton, "These forces of reaction feed on disillusionment, poverty and despair," and he advocates a socioeconomic remedy: "spread prosperity and security to all." Edward Djerejian, once a top State Department figure, reports that "political Islamic movements are to an important degree rooted in worsening socio-economic conditions in individual countries." Martin Indyk, another former high-ranking U.S. diplomat, warns that those wishing to reduce the appeal of militant Islam must first solve the economic, social and political problems that constitute its breeding grounds.

Militant Islam reflects "the economic, political, and cultural disappointment" of Muslims, according to former German Foreign Minister Klaus Kinkel. Former Interior Minister Charles Pasqua of France finds that this phenomenon "has coincided with despair on the part of a large section of the masses, and young people in particular." Prime Minister Eddie Fenech of Malta draws an even closer tie: "Fundamentalism grows at the same pace as economic problems." Israel's Foreign Minister Shimon Peres flatly asserts that "fundamentalism's basis is poverty" and that it offers "a way of protesting against poverty, corruption, ignorance, and discrimination."

Armed with this theory of cause and effect, businessmen on occasion make investments with an eye to political amelioration. The Virgin Group's chairman, Richard Branson, declared as he opened a music store in Beirut: "The region will become stable if people invest in it, create jobs and rebuild the countries that need rebuilding, not ignore them."

Poverty Is Not a Factor

But the empirical record evinces little correlation between economics and militant Islam. Aggregate measures of wealth and economic trends fall flat as predictors of where militant Islam will be strong and where not. On the level of individuals, too, conventional wisdom points to militant Islam attracting the poor, the alienated and the marginal—but research finds precisely the opposite to be true. To the extent that economic factors explain who becomes Islamist, they point to the fairly well off, not the poor. . . .

Even Islamists who make the ultimate sacrifice and give up their lives fit this pattern of financial ease and advanced education. A disproportionate number of terrorists and suicide bombers have higher education, often in engineering and the sciences. This generalization applies equally to the Palestinian suicide bombers attacking Israel and the followers of Osama bin Laden who hijacked the four planes of September 11. In the first case, one researcher found by looking at their profiles that: "Economic circumstances did not seem to be a decisive factor. While none of the 16 subjects could be described as well-off, some were certainly struggling less than others." In the second case, as the Princeton historian Sean Wilentz sardonically put it, the biographies of the September 11 killers would imply that the root cause of terrorism is "money, education and privilege." More generally, Fathi ash-Shiqaqi, founding leader of the arch-murderous Islamic Jihad, once commented, "Some of the young people who have sacrificed themselves [in terrorist operations] came from well-off families and had successful university careers." This makes sense, for suicide bombers who hurl themselves against foreign enemies offer their lives not to protest financial deprivation but to change the world.

Hatred, Not Poverty

Suggesting that poverty breeds terrorism is disingenuous at best. Hatred breeds terrorism. By all accounts, [terrorist] Osama bin Laden is a very wealthy man—how else could he self-finance a global terrorist network and elude the world's most powerful military and law enforcement agencies for over six months?

Thomas P. Kilgannon, "Monterrey Madness," April 8, 2002. http://www. freedomalliance.org.

Those who back militant Islamic organizations also tend to be well off. They come more often from the richer city than the poorer countryside, a fact that, as Khalid M. Amayreh, a Palestinian journalist, points out, "refutes the widely-held assumption that Islamist popularity thrives on economic misery." And they come not just from the cities but from the upper ranks. At times, an astonishing one-quarter of the membership in Turkey's leading militant Islamic organization, now called the Saadet Party, have been engineers. Indeed, the typical cadre in a militant Islamic party is an engineer in his forties born in a city to parents who had moved from the countryside. . . .

Not a Product of Poverty

The same pattern that holds for individual Islamists exists on the level of societies, as well. That social pattern can be expressed by four propositions.

First, wealth does not inoculate against militant Islam. Kuwaitis enjoy a Western-style income (and owe their state's very existence to the West) but Islamists generally win the largest bloc of seats in parliament (at present, twenty out of fifty). The West Bank is more prosperous than Gaza, yet militant Islamic groups usually enjoy more popularity in the former than the latter. Militant Islam flourishes in the member states of the European Union and in North America, where Muslims as a group enjoy a standard of living higher than the national averages. And of those Muslims, as Khalid Duran points out, Islamists have the generally higher incomes: "In the United States, the difference between Islamists and common Muslims is largely one between haves and have-nots. Muslims have the numbers; Islamists have the dollars."

Second, a flourishing economy does not inoculate against radical Islam. Today's militant Islamic movements took off in the 1970s, precisely as oil-exporting states enjoyed extraordinary growth rates. Muammar Qaddafi developed his eccentric version of proto-militant Islam then; fanatical groups in Saudi Arabia violently seized the Great Mosque of Mecca; and Ayatollah Khomeini took power in Iran (though, admittedly, growth had slacked off several years before he overthrew the Shah). In the 1980s, several countries that excelled economically experienced a militant Islamic boom. Jordan, Tunisia and Morocco all did well economically in the 1990s—as did their militant Islamic movements. Turks under Turgut Özal enjoyed nearly a decade of particularly impressive economic growth even as they joined militant Islamic parties in ever larger numbers.

Third, poverty does not generate militant Islam. There are many very poor Muslim states but few of them have become centers of militant Islam—not Bangladesh, not Yemen, and not Niger. As an American specialist rightly notes, "economic despair, the oft-cited source of political Islam's power, is familiar to the Middle East"; if militant Islam is connected to poverty, why was it not a stronger force in years and centuries past, when the region was poorer than it is today?

Fourth, a declining economy does not generate militant Islam. The 1997 crash in Indonesia and Malaysia did not spur a large turn toward militant Islam. Iranian incomes have gone down by half or more since the Islamic Republic came to power in 1979; yet, far from increasing support for the regime's militant Islamic ideology, impoverishment has caused a massive alienation from Islam. Iraqis have experienced an even more precipitous drop in living standards: [Economics professor] Abbas Alnasrawi estimates that per capita income has plummeted by nearly 90 percent since 1980, returning it to where it was in the 1940s. While the country has witnessed an increase in personal piety, militant Islam has not surged, nor is it the leading expression of anti-regime sentiments.

Noting these patterns, at least a few observers have drawn the correct conclusion. The outspoken Algerian secularist, Saïd Sadi, flatly rejects the thesis that poverty spurs militant Islam: "I do not adhere to this view that it is widespread unemployment and poverty which produce terrorism." Likewise, Amayreh finds that militant Islam "is not a product or by-product of poverty.". . .

Wealth Breeds Revolution

If poverty is not the driving force behind militant Islam, several policy implications follow. First, prosperity cannot be looked to as the solution to militant Islam and foreign aid cannot serve as the outside world's main tool to combat it. Second, Westernization also does not provide a solution. To the contrary, many outstanding militant Islamic leaders are not just familiar with Western ways but are expert in them. In particular, a disproportionate number of them have advanced degrees in technology and the sciences. It sometimes seems that Westernization is a route to hating the West. Third, economic growth does not inevitably lead to improved relations with Muslim states. In some cases (for example, Algeria), it might help; in others (Saudi Arabia), it might hurt.

Could it be, quite contrarily, that militant Islam results from wealth rather than poverty? It is possible. There is, after all, the universal phenomenon that people become more engaged ideologically and active politically only when they have reached a fairly high standard of living. Revolutions take place, it has often been noted, only when a substantial middle class exists. Birthe Hansen, an associate professor at the University of Copenhagen, hints at this when she writes that "the spread of free market capitalism and liberal democracy . . . is probably an important factor behind the rise of political Islam."

Moreover, there is a specifically Islamic phenomenon of the faith having been associated with worldly success. Through history, from the Prophet Muhammad's time to the Ottoman Empire a millennium later, Muslims usually had more wealth and more power than other peoples, and were more literate and healthy. With time, Islamic faith came to be associated with worldly well-being—a kind of Muslim Calvinism, in effect. This connection appears still to hold. For example, as noted in the formulation known as Issawi's law ("Where there are Muslims, there is oil; the converse is not true"), the 1970s oil boom mainly benefited Muslims; it is probably no coincidence that the current wave of militant Islam began then. Seeing themselves as "pioneers of a movement that is an alternative to Western civilization," Islamists need a strong economic base. As Galal Amin writes, "There may be a strong relationship between the growth of incomes that have the nature of economic rent and the growth of religious fanaticism."

Conversely, poor Muslims have tended to be more impressed by alternative affiliations. Over the centuries, for example, apostasy from the religion has mostly occurred when things have gone badly. That was the case when Tatars fell under Russian rule or when Sunni Lebanese lost power to the Maronites. It was also the case in 1995 in Iraqi Kurdistan, a region under double embargo and suffering from civil war:

> Trying to live their lives in the midst of fire and gunpowder, Kurdish villagers have reached the point where they are prepared to give up anything to save themselves from hunger and death. From their perspective, changing their religion to get a visa to the West is becoming an increasingly more important option.

There are, in short, ample reasons for thinking that militant Islam results more from success than from failure.

"Military action is [Hamas's] strategic instrument for combating the Zionist element."

Israel's Occupation of Palestine Causes Terrorism

Hamas

Military action by Palestinians is the result of the Israeli (Zionist) occupation of Muslim lands, the militant organization Hamas asserts in the following viewpoint. Hamas contends that Israel aims to undermine Palestine's economic, political, and military power and is a threat to the Arab world. The organization maintains that military action (which many in the West call terrorism) is a necessary tool in the fight to end the Israeli occupation and liberate Palestine "from the river to the sea." Hamas concludes that all governments, not only Arab and Islamic ones, should aid the organization in the achievement of that goal. "Hamas" is the Arabic acronym for the Islamic Resistance Movement, a radical Islamic organization that seeks to replace Israel with a Palestinian state.

As you read, consider the following questions:

1. In Hamas's view, what is Israel's objective?
2. According to Hamas, what is the best way to respond to the conflict with Israel?
3. Why should Hamas resistance not be associated with the peace process, according to the author?

Hamas, "Hamas—In Their Own Words," www.palestine-info.com, 2002.

Hamas is an acronym that stands for the Islamic Resistance Movement, a popular national resistance movement which is working to create conditions conducive to emancipating the Palestinian people, delivering them from tyranny, liberating their land from the occupying usurper, and to stand up to the Zionist scheme which is supported by neo-colonist forces.

Hamas is a Jihadi (fighting for a holy purpose) movement in the broad sense of the word Jihad. It is part of the Islamic awakening movement and upholds that this awakening is the road which will lead to the liberation of Palestine from the [Jordan] river to the [Mediterranean] sea. It is also a popular movement in the sense that it is a practical manifestation of a wide popular current that is deeply rooted in the ranks of the Palestinian people and the Islamic nation. It is a current which sees in the Islamic faith and doctrines a firm base in which to work against an enemy which endorses religious ideologies and plots which counteract all plans to lift up the Palestinian nation. The Hamas movement groups in its ranks all those who believe in its ideology and principles and all who are prepared to endure the consequences of the conflict and to confront the Zionist scheme. . . .

An Antagonistic Regime

The Hamas movement believes that the conflict with the Zionists in Palestine is a conflict of survival. It is a conflict of civilization and determination that can not be brought to an end unless its cause—the Zionist settlement in Palestine, usurpation of its land, and the displacement of its people—is removed.

Hamas sees in the Hebraic state an antagonistic totalitarian regime, not just an entity with territorial ambitions, a regime that complements the forces of modern colonialism which aim to take hold of the nation's riches and resources and to prevent the rise of any grouping that works to unify the nation's ranks. It seeks to achieve this objective by promoting provincialisms, alienating the nation from its cultural roots and clamping down on its economic, political, military and even intellectual hegemony.

The Hebraic state forms an instrument that breaks the

geographic continuity of the central Arab countries, and it is a device to deplete the nation's resources. It is also a spearhead which is ready to strike at any project that aims to raise the nation up.

The Advantage of Suicide Bombings

In terms of technological feasibility, suicide bombings present several obvious advantages. Besides the fact that bombs can be constructed fairly easily from widely available components such as ammonium nitrate, acetone, and nitrogen glycerin, the Hamas military wing, Izzadin al Qassam, has already demonstrated a high level of bomb-making proficiency. These factors, along with the relative ease with which an explosive can be delivered via a human carrier, make this tactic very attractive from a technological standpoint.

A suicide bomber has the ability to deliver the payload to places otherwise inaccessible to those trying to stay alive. The fact that he or she also has the ability to choose the exact location, time, and circumstances of the attack results in the striking effectiveness of suicidal bombings in terms of delivering a high number of casualties. Suicide attacks are also attractive because they do not require the planning of an escape route, and they nearly eliminate the danger of capture and subsequent interrogation.

Adam Dolnik and Anjali Bhattacharjee, *Terrorism and Political Violence*, Autumn 2002.

The main confrontations with the Zionist entity is taking place in Palestine where the enemy has established its base and stronghold. But the threats and challenges posed by the Zionists run deeper and so threaten all Islamic countries. Hamas believes that the Zionist entity, since its inception, has constituted a threat to the Arab countries and also in their strategic depth, the Islamic countries. The 90s witnessed huge transformations that highlighted this danger which knows no limits.

Hamas believes that the best way to handle the conflict with the Zionist enemy is to mobilize the potentialities of the Palestinian people in the struggle against the Zionist presence in Palestine and to keep the firebrand burning until the time when the conditions to win the battle have been realized, and wait until all the potentialities and resources of the

Arab and Islamic nation are mobilized under a common political will and purpose. Until that happens and there is belief in the sanctity of the Palestinian cause and its Islamic importance and an awareness of the ultimate goals and dangers of the Zionist project in Palestine, Hamas believes that no part of Palestine should be compromised, that the Zionist occupation of Palestine should not be recognized and that it is imperative for the people of Palestine, as well as all Arabs and Muslims, to prepare themselves to fight the Zionists until they leave Palestine the way they migrated to it.

Reasons for Military Action

The Hebraic state represents an entity which is antagonistic to all aims of Arab and Islamic awakening, for it is known that had it not been for the state of deterioration and decadence through which the nation was passing, the Zionists would not have realized their dream of establishing their state in Palestine.

Recognizing this fact, the Zionists work against any program which they think would add to the Arab and Islamic capabilities. They believe that any attempts aiming at achieving an Arab and Islamic awakening constitute a strategic threat to Israel. The Zionists also believe that if Arab power was unified under a comprehensive program of awakening, it would pose a major threat to the Hebraic state. This conviction has prompted the Zionist leaders to transform their state from an alien entity in the Arab and Islamic surrounding to become part of it under the influence of economy. This explains why they support the (peace) settlement and promote projects with an economic orientation. It is within this context that the military action in the Hamas program should be viewed. Military action is the movement's strategic instrument for combating the Zionist element. In the absence of a comprehensive Arab and Islamic plan for liberation, military action will remain the only guarantee that would keep the conflict going and that would make it difficult for the enemy to expand outside Palestine.

Hamas believes that Israel's integration into the Arab and Islamic region would hamper every plan that seeks to uplift the nation.

Hamas resistance against the occupation is not directed against the Jews as followers of a religion, but rather against the occupation, its existence and oppressive practices. This resistance is not associated with the peace process in the region as alleged by the Hebraic state and the supporters of the current settlement. The resistance was there before the convening of the Madrid Conference,[1] and the movement has no hostilities or battles with any international party, nor does it target the interests of the properties of the various countries. This is because it considers that the scene of its battle against the Zionist occupation is limited to the Occupied Palestinian territories. When the Zionist officials threatened to transfer the battle with Hamas to areas outside the Occupied Territories, Hamas warned the Zionist authorities against the serious dangers of such a step. This testifies to the fact that Hamas does not wish to enlarge the circle of the conflict.

External Relations

1. Hamas believes that the difference in opinions over developments does not prevent it from contacting and cooperating with amiable parties that are prepared to support the steadfastness of the Palestinian people.

2. Hamas is not interested in the internal affairs of countries and does not interfere in any government's domestic affairs.

3. Hamas seeks to encourage Arab and Islamic countries to resolve their differences and to unify their attitudes towards national issues. However, it does not side with one party against the other, nor does it accept joining one political axis against another.

4. Hamas believes in Arab and Islamic unity and blesses any effort made in this respect.

5. Hamas asks all Arab and Islamic governments and parties to assume their responsibilities to endorse the cause of our people and support its steadfastness against the Zionist occupation and to facilitate the work of our movement to-

1. The Madrid Conference, held in November 1991, marked the beginning of the Arab-Israeli peace process. Israel, Lebanon, Syria, and a joint Jordanian-Palestinian delegation participated.

wards achieving its mission.

6. Hamas believes in the importance of dialogue with all governments and world parties and forces irrespective of faith, race or political orientation. It remains ready to cooperate with any side for the sake of the just cause of our people and for informing the public about the inhuman practices of the Zionist occupation against the Palestine people.

7. Hamas does not seek enmity with anyone on the basis of religious convictions or race. It does not antagonize any country or organization unless they stand against our people or support the aggressive practices of the Zionist occupation against our people.

8. Hamas is keen on limiting the theater of confrontation with the Zionist occupation to Palestine, and not to transfer it to any arena outside Palestine.

9. Hamas expects the world's countries, organizations and liberty movements to stand by the just cause of our people; to denounce the repressive practices of the occupation authorities which violate international law and human rights; and to create a public opinion pressurizing the Zionist entity to end its occupation of our land and holy shrines.

"The problem [of Palestinian Arabs] is their ideology of hatred for Jews."

Palestinian Hatred of Israel Causes Terrorism

Morton A. Klein

In the following viewpoint Morton A. Klein asserts that hatred of Jews and the state of Israel causes Palestinian terrorism against Israelis. He disputes the claim that poverty in Palestinian territories leads to terrorism, arguing that most of the terrorists are university-educated professionals. Instead, Klein asserts that Palestinians and fellow Arabs have targeted Israel for ideological reasons. According to Klein, because the cause of Palestinian terrorism is religious and political in nature, America should realize that an economic solution to Middle East peace is destined to fail. Klein is the president of the Zionist Organization of America, which supports pro-Israel legislation and aims to strengthen American-Israeli relations.

As you read, consider the following questions:

1. How much money has the United States given to Palestinian Arabs since 1994, according to Klein?
2. In the author's opinion, what was the impact of Jewish immigration to Palestine in the 1920s and 1930s?
3. According to Amos Perlmutter, who are the leaders of the terrorist group Hamas?

It is widely assumed that poverty is a prime factor in motivating Palestinian Arabs to become terrorists—that material deprivation makes young Arabs feel desperate, which leads them to terrorism. This theory is the reasoning behind the nearly $1 billion the U.S. has given to the Palestinian Arabs since 1994, and the even larger amounts that the European Union has given them. These governments claim that if young Arabs have jobs, they would have something to lose by becoming terrorists, so they would have a strong incentive to maintain normal, peaceful lives.

In fact, however, many of the leading Palestinian Arab terrorists—including some suicide bombers—are university graduates, are married, and have good jobs. Consider one example from many: Muhammad Abu Jamous, who was part of a terror squad that murdered four Israelis in Gaza on January 9, 2002. According to the *New York Times*, Abu Jamous was "a member of the Palestinian Navy [and] something of a minor celebrity. He had been a runner on the Palestinian national team, competing in Egypt and Saudi Arabia. He married just three months ago, and his wife is two months pregnant." In other words, he had everything to lose. He had a good job. He was even something of a celebrity. He was a newlywed, and his wife is already expecting a child. He had every logical reason to live peacefully and quietly. Yet he picked up a gun and went out to murder innocent Israelis.

Money Is Not the Issue

The Palestinian Arabs know that if they made peace with Israel, their economy would improve dramatically, as would their material lives. Yet they continue to wage war against Israel—because the problem is not the economy. The problem is their ideology of hatred for Jews and refusal to accept the existence of a Jewish State in their midst. An editorial in the *Jerusalem Post* once pointed out that

> there is no reason to believe that money would . . . persuade Palestinians to coexist with Israel . . . not all problems can be solved with money . . . Americans are particularly aware of the limitations of financial aid in resolving social and political problems. Throwing staggering amounts of government and private funds at inner-city slums, the drug problem and affirmative action for minorities had done little to ameliorate

Early Examples of Palestinian Terrorism

- July 22, 1968: Three members of the Popular Front for the Liberation of Palestine hijack an El Al flight from Rome. All hostages are released safely.
- September 4, 1968: One civilian is killed and seventy-one are injured when three bombs explode in central Tel Aviv.
- November 22, 1968: An Al-Fateh bombing of a market in Israel kills twelve people and injures fifty-two.
- February 21, 1970: Palestinian terrorists blow up a Swissair jet bound for Tel Aviv. All forty-seven people on board are killed.
- September 5, 1972: A Palestine Liberation Organization (PLO) faction murders eleven Israeli athletes and coaches at the Summer Olympics in Munich. Five terrorists die and three are captured in a firefight with German sharpshooters. An Israeli assassination squad eventually kills two of the surviving terrorists.

Alan M. Dershowitz, *Why Terrorism Works*, 2002.

intractable problems. It is even less likely that the Arab-Israeli conflict can be reduced to materialist terms. The intolerance in the Arab world for Israel's existence does not stem from economic hardship. It is mostly religiously and nationalistically inspired.

The historical record clearly demonstrates that Arab extremist ideology, rather than poverty, is at the core of the Arab-Jewish conflict. During the 1920s and 1930s, for example, Jewish immigration to Palestine brought the country a variety of economic improvements, including new jobs for many Arabs—yet there was mass Palestinian Arab violence against Jews in 1920, 1921, 1929, and throughout 1936–1939. Nor were the Arab wars against Israel (1948, 1956, 1967, 1973) fought for economic reasons. Nor was the constant Palestinian Arab terrorism against Israel during the 1950s, 1960s, 1970s, 1980s, and 1990s motivated by economic troubles. Whether in good economic times or bad, the Arabs remained committed to murdering Jews and seeking Israel's destruction.

Devoted to an Ideology

The ranks of the current Palestinian Arab terrorist groups have been filled by a generation of radical young Arab nationalists, many of them university-educated (Israel built six universities, and sixteen other institutions of higher education, in Judea-Samaria-Gaza) and relatively well-to-do, who organized mass violence for ideological, not economic, reasons. As the late professor Amos Perlmutter once pointed out, the leadership of the Hamas terrorist movement—which supplies the suicide bombers—"is made up of modern middle- and upper-middle class professionals, of journalists, lawyers, engineers and doctors." Indeed, news accounts of the 400 Hamas leaders who were temporarily deported to Lebanon in 1992–1993, described the deportees as well-educated professionals. Building factories or hospitals will not put an end to hatred of Israel. Devoted to ideologies of extreme Arab nationalism or extremist Islam, the Palestinian Arabs reject the concept of a sovereign non-Muslim state in the Muslim Middle East. Giving them American taxpayers' dollars won't change that.

Periodical Bibliography

The following articles have been selected to supplement the diverse views presented in this chapter.

David Gelernter "They Hate Us Because They Hate Israel," *Wall Street Journal*, October 8, 2001.

Sohail Hashmi "Don't Say It Was Religious," *Washington Post National Weekly Edition*, October 8–14, 2001.

Hussein Ibish "Occupation Propels Conflict," *Los Angeles Times*, December 4, 2001.

Bernard Lewis "Jihad vs. Crusade," *Wall Street Journal*, September 27, 2001.

Sheryl McCarthy "Americans Need to Understand Reasons for Attack," *Liberal Opinion Week*, October 1, 2001.

Daniel Pipes "The Danger Within: Militant Islam in America," *Commentary*, November 2001.

Jeremy Rabkin "Sovereignty Amidst Terror," *Weekly Standard*, October 1, 2001.

Barry Rubin "The Real Roots of Arab Anti-Americanism," *Foreign Affairs*, November/December 2002.

David Schafer "Islam and Terrorism: A Humanist View," *Humanist*, May/June 2002.

Stephen R. Shalom "Confronting Terrorism and War," *New Politics*, Winter 2002.

Mark Steyn "They Want to Kill Us All," *Spectator*, October 19, 2002.

Antony T. Sullivan "Should Policymakers See Islam as an Enemy of the West? No: Islam, Judaism, and Christianity Historically Produce Societies with Like Characteristics," *Insight on the News*, November 5, 2001.

Shibley Telhami "Why Suicide Terrorism Takes Root," *New York Times*, April 4, 2002.

Shashi Tharoor "India's Past Becomes a Weapon," *New York Times*, March 6, 2002.

Robert W. Tracinski "The Three Wars of World War III," *Intellectual Activist*, November 2001.

Reshma Memon Yaqub "I'm Not the Enemy," *Washington Post National Weekly Edition*, September 17–23, 2001.

CHAPTER 3

How Should America's Domestic War on Terrorism Be Conducted?

Chapter Preface

On September 11, 2001, four sets of pilots and copilots were overcome by terrorists who stormed the cockpits of passenger liners and turned the planes into massive bombs, acts that would lead to three thousand deaths, the destruction of New York City's Twin Towers, and significant damage to the Pentagon. In the wake of that day's horrors, many people have begun to wonder if future terrorist acts could be thwarted by giving pilots guns so they could protect their planes against hijackers.

The debate about arming pilots heightened in the summer and fall of 2002. On July 10, 2002, the House of Representatives passed House Resolution 4635, the Arming Pilots Against Terrorism Act, by a 310-113 vote. The House's action was promptly criticized by the Violence Policy Center (VPC), a pro–gun control organization. In a press release, the VPC contended that providing pilots with guns would raise a host of problems. Among the concerns raised by the center were that terrorists would use the guns against the pilots and that guns could be discharged accidentally. In addition, the organization asserts, "When police fire their weapons, they sometimes make grave mistakes in deciding when deadly force is justified. It is naive to believe that pilots will perform any better." Other critics of the proposal caution that a misfired bullet could go through the hull of the aircraft and cause depressurization, making it difficult for the pilots to safely fly and land the plane.

Advocates of arming pilots have countered these concerns. In an editorial that appeared on the *National Review Online* website on September 6, 2002, Doug Bandow, a fellow at the Cato Institute, a libertarian think tank, argued in favor of arming pilots and noted that many of the fears of anti-gun organizations can readily be allayed. For example, "smart" guns, which can only be fired by preprogrammed users, would eliminate the ability of terrorists to use guns they wrested from pilots. Accidental discharge or other gun-handling mistakes are also unlikely, Bandow points out, because many pilots were once in the military and have thus been trained to handle and discharge weapons. Bandow also claims that planes can still be flown safely even after significant structural damage from a bullet hole. Syndicated columnist Stephen Chapman maintains that the greatest advantage of providing pilots with guns is not that they would shoot hijackers but that the knowledge a pilot is armed would deter potential terrorists.

The legislative debate on arming pilots ended on November 25, 2002, when H.R. 5005—a bill that established the Department of Homeland Security—became law. That bill incorporated H.R. 4635. In April 2003 the Transportation Security Administration (TSA), which operates as part of the Department of Homeland Security, began training commercial airline pilots who wanted to learn how to defend their planes. According to a press release issued by the TSA, the pilots who were psychologically, cognitively, and physically qualified would learn "firearms instruction, defensive tactics and information on how to transport their service weapons." Twice-yearly recertification is also required.

Arming pilots is one of the steps the United States has taken in its domestic war on terrorism. In the following chapter the contributors evaluate the benefits and drawbacks of several antiterrorism policies. Whether these policies will successfully protect America remains to be seen.

"The Patriot Act revised outdated rules that fatally hampered surveillance of suspected terrorists in America."

Antiterrorism Legislation Will Make America Safer

Michelle Malkin

In the following viewpoint Michelle Malkin contends that the USA PATRIOT Act—legislation passed on October 5, 2001, that expanded the surveillance powers of domestic law enforcement and international intelligence agencies—will make America safer in the wake of the September 11, 2001, terrorist attacks. She maintains that the act has already thwarted further acts of terror by helping law enforcement break up terror cells, convict people guilty of terror-related crimes, and prevent foreign criminals and terrorists from entering the United States. Malkin concludes that the USA PATRIOT Act will continue to achieve similar triumphs without destroying civil liberties. Malkin is a syndicated columnist and the author of *Invasion: How America Still Welcomes Terrorists, Criminals, and Other Foreign Menaces to Our Shores.*

As you read, consider the following questions:

1. How many immigrants have been deported after being linked to the September 11 investigation, according to Malkin?
2. According to the author, to whom have "civil liberties alarmists" compared Attorney General John Ashcroft?
3. In Edmund Burke's opinion what must first be achieved in order for liberty to be exercised?

Michelle Malkin, "Be Grateful for Patriot Act," *Human Events*, July 14, 2003, p. 10. Copyright © 2003 by *Human Events*. Reproduced by permission.

To civil liberties alarmists, Viet Dinh is a traitor. To me, he is an American hero.

Dinh, 35, is widely known—and reviled—as the primary architect of the Patriot Act. Until May [2003], he was an assistant attorney general for the Office of Legal Policy in John Ashcroft's Justice Department. (He stepped down to return to his law school post at Georgetown University.)

Since the September 11 [2001] terrorist attacks, Dinh told *The Christian Science Monitor*, "our nation's ability to defend itself against terror has been not only my vocation but my obsession."

Tranquility, Defense, and Liberty

This past Fourth of July holiday [in 2003], I thanked those like Dinh who have worked tirelessly to ensure domestic tranquility, provide for the common defense, and secure the blessings of liberty that no other country in the world can match.

A constitutional law expert, Dinh's office had been mostly concerned with judicial nominations before September 11. After the mass murder of 3,000 men, women and children on American soil, Dinh became an instrumental member of the brain trust that designed the Bush Administration's anti-terrorism policies.

Most importantly, the Patriot Act revised outdated rules that fatally hampered surveillance of suspected terrorists in America. Dinh also helped craft plans to monitor the entry and exit of foreign students and to register and track non-immigrant visitors from high-risk Middle Eastern countries.

An immigrant himself who escaped from communist Vietnam a quarter-century ago aboard a rickety boat, Dinh notes that foreign visitors to our shores are guests obligated to obey the laws—some which "have not been enforced for 50 years." It was time, Dinh and his colleagues decided, to start enforcing them.

Positive Results

The results speak for themselves:
- The feds have busted more than 20 suspected al Qaeda[1]

---

1. Al Qaeda was the terrorist network behind the September 11, 2001, attacks.

Catching Up with Technology

Believe it or not, before 9/11 the regulations that allowed public authorities to record or trace e-mail were interpreted by Department of Justice lawyers as requiring a court order from every jurisdiction through which an e-mail message traveled. This was a holdover from the days when phone lines were local; warrants for phone taps were granted by local authorities and had only a local reach. But today, e-mail messages zoom around by a variety of routes. Now, thanks to the Patriot Act, nationwide tracing and recording orders are permitted under FISA [Foreign Intelligence Surveillance Act]. That is, law enforcement authorities may finally catch up with the technological features of e-mail. Anybody who sees a civil rights violation here should have his vision checked.

Amitai Etzioni, *Weekly Standard*, July 21, 2003.

---

cell members from Buffalo, N.Y., to Detroit, Seattle, and Portland, Ore.

• More than 100 other individuals have been convicted or pled guilty to terrorist-related crimes.

• The United States has deported 515 individuals linked to the September 11 investigation.

• Hundreds of foreign criminals and suspected terrorists, plus one known member of al Qaeda, were prevented from entering the country thanks to the National Entry-Exit Registration System—which Sen. Ted Kennedy (D.-Mass.) attempted to sabotage earlier this year [2003].

• Long overdue fingerprint cross checks of immigration and FBI databases at the border have resulted in the arrest of more than 5,000 fugitives wanted for crimes committed in the United States.

• And nearly two years after the September 11 attacks, there has not yet been another mass terrorist attack on our homeland.

No Threat to Civil Liberties

Opponents of the Bush Administration's homeland defense and immigration enforcement efforts complain that the war on terror has eviscerated civil liberties and constitutional rights.

They have falsely portrayed the Patriot Act as allowing the

feds to spy on library patrons without a warrant or criminal suspicion—a lie perpetuated by the truth-challenged *New York Times*. They have hysterically compared the detention of illegal aliens from terror-friendly countries to the World War II internment of Japanese.

And they have likened Ashcroft, Dinh, and the Justice Department to the [former Afghanistan government] Taliban and Nazis.

Never mind that the courts have so far upheld every major initiative and tactic from keeping immigration deportation hearings closed, to maintaining secrecy of the names of illegal alien detainees, to allowing use of the Patriot Act surveillance powers.

Dinh is refreshingly unapologetic and to the point in response to the alarmists: "The threat to liberty comes from Osama bin Laden and his [al Qaeda] terrorist network, not from the men and women in blue who work to uphold the law."

Drawing on [political philosopher] Edmund Burke's theory of "Ordered Liberty," which argues that liberty cannot be exercised unless government has first provided civil order, Dinh observes: "I think security exists for liberty to flourish and liberty cannot exist without order and security."

On July 4, this fundamental lesson of September 11 must not be forgotten. The charred earth, mangled steel, crashing glass, fiery chaos and eviscerated bodies are indelible reminders that the blessings of liberty in America do not secure themselves.

"The USA PATRIOT Act [is] a bill that twists the assumptions contained in the Bill of Rights."

Antiterrorism Legislation Threatens Civil Liberties

Hank Kalet

On October 5, 2001—less than four weeks after the September 11 terrorist attacks—Congress passed the USA PATRIOT Act, a law that significantly expands the surveillance powers of America's domestic law enforcement and international intelligence agencies. The law's passage, along with other actions taken by the Bush administration, will threaten the civil liberties and freedoms to which Americans are entitled, Hank Kalet opines in the following viewpoint. According to Kalet, the USA PATRIOT Act ignores Americans' rights to due process and privacy while also aiming to stifle speech that criticizes the government. Kalet maintains that freedom must not be relinquished in exchange for security because that may lead to the end of the United States as a democratic republic. Kalet is the managing editor of two newspapers in New Jersey, the *South Brunswick Post* and the *Cranbury Press.*

As you read, consider the following questions:

1. What is "preventative detention," as explained by the author?
2. According to Kalet, why did Sidney Hook write his essay "Bread and Freedom"?
3. What kind of war is the United States involved in, as quoted by Ted Galen Carpenter?

Hank Kalet, "Remember 9/11 by Protecting Democracy," *Progressive Populist*, September 1, 2002, p. 13. Copyright © 2002 by *Progressive Populist*. Reproduced by permission.

To quote Thomas Paine, author of the Revolutionary War pamphlets *The American Crisis* and *Common Sense*, "These are the times that try men's souls."

The freedoms we hold dear are under attack—and I'm not talking about by [terrorist network] Al-Qaeda. I'm talking about by the Bush administration and Congress.

In the year since 19 terrorists hijacked four planes and flew three into the World Trade Center and Pentagon [on September 11, 2001], as America mourned the 3,000 or so who died and fretted over the dangers of what many perceive as a drastically different world, the Bush administration has moved to consolidate federal power, enhancing the authority of law enforcement while removing much of what it has done or plans to do from judicial oversight.

A Consolidation of Power

The short list is fairly compelling:

It has placed at least two Americans under indefinite detention without charges or attorneys, claiming that they worked with the al-Qaeda terror network and therefore forfeited the constitutional protections the rest of us enjoy.

It has rounded up and kept secret the names of hundreds of foreign-born individuals, most without charges or access to legal representations, in what has [been] called "preventative detention," essentially replaying our detention of Japanese-Americans during World War II. In conjunction, it has closed hearings in what the nation's chief immigration judge has called "special interest" immigration cases and closed off access to the federal courts for aliens who wish to challenge this secrecy. (A federal judge has ruled that the administration has to release the names. . . .)

Congress, under cover of night and with the full support of the Bush administration, passed the USA PATRIOT Act, a bill that twists the assumptions contained in the Bill of Rights, unleashing law enforcement authorities to ignore issues of privacy and due process by legalizing roving wiretaps and covert searches and to target dissent through its broad definition of terrorism.

The Bill of Rights, of course, is supposed to guarantee us the right to speak freely and to assemble and seek "a redress of grievances." It is supposed to protect us from unreasonable searches and seizures by police, without "probable cause, supported by Oath or affirmation, and particularly describing the place to be searched, and the persons or things to be seized." And it is supposed to require that those arrested and accused of crimes be guaranteed due process of law, an attorney and the right to confront their accusers.

Freedom Versus Security

Attorney General John Ashcroft and his supporters—and the majority of Americans, according to the poll numbers—say we have to be willing to relinquish some of our freedoms temporarily to ensure our safety and security in this time of war.

Not everyone agrees. Judge Gladys Kessler of Federal District Court in Washington pointedly criticized the administration, saying, "secret arrests are a concept odious to a democratic society." She wrote that "the public's interest in learning the identity of those arrested and detained is essential to verifying whether the government is operating within the bounds of law."

Not according to the Justice Department, which says the judicial branch has little right to intervene in the conduct of war. And most Americans seem to support the Justice Department and the Bush administration, according to a *Washington Post* poll.

It is easy to see why people might feel this way. Fear is a powerful emotion and most people believe that limitations on constitutional rights will have no effect on them, that only people with something to hide require the right to hide it.

Do Not Relinquish Freedom

But it's important to remember that these constitutional protections are the bedrock of our freedoms and that chipping away at them for safety's sake can have drastic consequences for all of us down the road.

The fact is, we cannot be secure unless we maintain our freedoms. The political philosopher Sidney Hook, in a 1940 essay called "Bread and Freedom," took to task those who would trade freedom for security—in his case, economic security.

"How can there be genuine security so long as arbitrary power, whether it be of an employer or a group, or especially of the state as employer, is not subject to the restraints of a freely operating democratic process?"

Sargent. © 2001 by Austin American Statesman. Reproduced by permission of Universal Press Syndicate.

Hook's essay was written in response to American communists, who were preaching that "bourgeois freedoms" were secondary and could be sacrificed to ensure that the proletariat achieves economic sufficiency. Being free to speak one's mind, to worship as one wished, to be free in one's house [was] thought to be less important than put[ting] food on the table or finding food and shelter.

Hook explained the danger of the tradeoff, saying that the only way to maintain freedom and security was to ensure that our core freedoms remain intact. These core freedoms—of speech and assembly, of inquiry and teaching, of press and other forms of communication, of cultural opportunity and development—are "what we should primarily mean by the American way of life," he wrote.

"For these are the strategic freedoms that enable us to win new freedoms and check the excesses of the old," he wrote. "So long as they prevail, modifications of and restrictions on other freedoms are reversible. Where they are undermined, no other freedom can be anything but an assertion of power by a privileged group."

A Permanent Tradeoff

And it's important to note that what we are calling a temporary tradeoff is likely to have a much longer shelf life than any of us realize today. The fact is, we are involved in a war against a "shadowy network of adversaries rather than a nation state," one that is likely to have no end, writes Ted Galen Carpenter of the Cato Institute, the libertarian think tank. Because of this, he says, it is likely that this tradeoff will become permanent, as well.

"We therefore need to ask whether we want to give not only the current president but also his unknown successors in the decades to come the awesome power that President [George W.] Bush has claimed," he wrote.

Allowing the national security state to grow unchecked is dangerous and potentially could alter the face of our nation, changing it from the democratic republic we have known into something very different.

That's not something we should pin on the 3,000 people who died on Sept. 11.

> *"Profiling is an aid—very far from an infallible one, but still a useful one—to identifying those who want to harm us."*

Racial Profiling Will Make America Safer

John Derbyshire

Racial profiling—when law enforcement uses race as a factor in determining which people pose a criminal threat—at airports will help America fight terrorism, John Derbyshire asserts in the following viewpoint. He contends that racial profiling could have thwarted the September 11, 2001, terrorist attacks. Derbyshire acknowledges that while it may sometimes be difficult to accurately identify Muslims of Middle Eastern origins (all the September 11 hijackers were Middle Eastern Muslims), airport officials must use profiling because it will help identify people who may intend to attack Americans. Derbyshire is a columnist for the *National Review* and a literary critic for several publications, including *New Criterion* and the *Washington Times*.

As you read, consider the following questions:

1. According to Derbyshire, what should be included in all emergency legislation before it can be enacted?
2. What proportion of Arab Americans are Christian, according to the author?
3. When did "of Middle Eastern appearance" (OMEA) profiling begin, according to Derbyshire?

John Derbyshire, "At First Glance," *National Review Online*, October 5, 2001.

Whether you think the present emergency rises to the level of a war or not, one thing that is fast becoming clear is that Americans at large are much more tolerant of racial profiling than they were before the terrorists struck [on September 11, 2001]. This fact was illustrated on September 20 [2001], when four men "of Middle Eastern appearance" were removed from a Northwest Airlines flight because other passengers refused to fly with them. A Northwest spokesman explained that under FAA [Federal Aviation Administration] rules, "the airline has no choice but to re-accommodate a passenger or passengers if their actions or presence make a majority of passengers uncomfortable and threaten to disrupt normal operations of flight."

Compare this incident with the experience of movie actor James Woods. Woods took a flight from Boston to Los Angeles one week before the World Trade Center attacks. The only other people in first class with him were four men "of Middle Eastern appearance" who acted very strangely. During the entire cross-country flight none of them had anything to eat or drink, nor did they read or sleep. They only sat upright in their seats, occasionally conversing with each other in low tones. Woods mentioned what he had noticed to a flight attendant, "who shrugged it off." Arriving in Los Angeles, Woods told airport authorities, but they "seemed unwilling to become involved."

Changing Attitudes

You can see the great change in our attitudes by imagining the consequences if the first incident had happened two weeks earlier, or the second two weeks later. The first would then have generated a nationwide storm of indignation about racial profiling, and stupendous lawsuits; the second, a huge police manhunt for the four men concerned. It seems very likely that Woods witnessed a dry run for the attack on the World Trade Center. One of the planes used in that attack was flying the same Boston–Los Angeles route that Woods flew. If the authorities had acted on his report—if, that is to say, they had been willing to entertain a little straightforward racial profiling—three thousand lives might have been saved.

Civil libertarians are now warning us that in the current climate of crisis and national peril, our ancient liberties might be sacrificed to the general desire for greater security. They have a point. If truth is the first casualty in war, liberty is often the second. The reason that practically nobody can afford to live in Manhattan who isn't already living there is rent control, a WWII measure, never repealed, that removed a landlord's freedom to let his property at whatever rent the market would bear. But the moral to be drawn from that instance is only that, as legal scholar Bruce Ackerman has recently argued, emergency legislation must never be enacted without a clear "sunset provision": After some fixed period—Ackerman suggests two years—the law must lapse. The civil-liberties crowd does not, in any case, have a dazzling record on the liberties involved in private commercial transactions. What happened to a cabdriver's liberty to use his own judgment about which passengers to pick up? Gone, swept away in the racial-profiling panic of the 1990s, along with the lives of several cabbies.

It is in the matter of proactive law enforcement—the kinds of things that police agencies do to prevent crime or terrorism—that our liberties are most at risk in tense times. Whom should you wiretap? Whom should airport security take in for questioning? This is where racial profiling kicks in, with all its ambiguities. Just take a careful look, for example, at that phrase "of Middle Eastern appearance," which I imagine security agencies are already abbreviating OMEA. The last time I wrote about this subject . . ., I concentrated on the topics that were in the air at that time: the disproportionate attention police officers give to black and Hispanic persons as crime suspects, and the targeting of Wen Ho Lee in [a] nuclear-espionage case. I had nothing to say about terrorists from the Middle East, or people who might be thought to look like them. OMEA was not, at that point, an issue.

Identity Confusion

Now it is, and the problem is that OMEA is perhaps a more dubious description even than "black" or "Hispanic." You can see the difficulties by scanning the photographs of the September 11 hijackers published in our newspapers. A few are unmistakably OMEA. My reaction on seeing the photograph of the first to be identified, Mohamed Atta, was that he looked exactly like my own mental conception of an Arab terrorist. On the other hand, one of his companions on AA Flight 11, Wail al-Shehri, is the spitting image of a boy I went to school with—a boy of entirely English origins, whose name was Hobson. Ahmed al-Nami (UA Flight 93) looks like a Welsh punk rocker. And so on.

FIND THE TERRORIST
(No Profiling Allowed)

Gorrell. © 2002 by Creators Syndicate, Inc. Reproduced by permission of Bob Gorrell.

Other visual markers offer similar opportunities for confusion. This fellow with a beard and a turban, coming down the road—he must surely be an Arab, or at least a Muslim? Well, maybe, but he is much more likely to be a Sikh—belonging, that is, to a religion that owes more to Hinduism than to Islam, practiced by non-Arab peoples who speak Indo-European languages, and with scriptures written with a Hindi-style script, not an Arabic one. Sikhism requires male adherents to keep an untrimmed beard and wear a turban; Islam does not.

Most other attempts at a "Middle Eastern" typology fail a lot of the time, too. Middle Easterners in the U.S. are mainly

Arabs, right? That depends on where you live. In the state of California, better than half are Iranian or Afghan; in Maryland, practically all are Iranian. Even if you restrict your attention to Americans of Arab origin, stereotypes quickly collapse. You would think it could at least be said with safety that they are mainly Muslims. Not so: More than three-quarters of Arab-Americans are Christians. The principal Middle Eastern presence in my own town is St. Mark's Coptic Church. The Copts, who are Egyptian Christians, are certainly OMEA, and they speak Arabic for non-liturgical purposes, and have Arabic names. They have little reason to identify with Muslim terrorists, however, having been rudely persecuted by extremist Muslims in their homeland for decades. Misconceptions cut the other way, too. Care to guess what proportion of Muslim Americans are of Arab origins? Answer: around one in eight. Most American Muslims are black.

That we could impose any even halfway reasonable system of "racial profiling" on this chaos seems impossible. Yet we can, where it matters most, and I believe we should; certainly in airport security, which, as a matter of fact, is where OMEA profiling began, during the hijack scares of the early 1970s. When boarding a plane, documents need to be presented, names declared, words exchanged. This gives security officials a much richer supply of data than a mere "eyeball" check. We return here to one of the points in my previous article on this subject, as affirmed by the U.S. Supreme Court: that "race"—which is to say, visible physical characteristics typical of, or at least frequent among, some groups with a common origin—can be used as part of a suspect profile to identify targets for further investigation, provided there are other criteria in play.

We should profile at airports because, as the James Woods incident shows, profiling is an aid—very far from an infallible one, but still a useful one—to identifying those who want to harm us, in this as in any other area of law enforcement. To pretend that any person passing through airport security is as likely as any other to be a hijacker is absurd, just as it is absurd to pretend that any driver on the New Jersey Turnpike is as likely as any other to be transporting narcotics. Crises like the present one can generate hysteria, it is true, but they can also have a clarifying effect on our outlook, sweeping away the wishful thinking of easier times, exposing the hollowness of relativism and moral equivalence, and forcing us to the main point. And peacetime has its own hysterias. I believe that when the long peace that ended on September 11 comes into perspective we shall see that the fuss about racial profiling was, ultimately, hysterical, driven by a dogmatic and unreasoned refusal to face up to group differences. So long as the authorities treat everyone with courtesy and apologize to the inconvenienced innocent, racial profiling is a practical and perfectly sensible tool for preventing crime and terrorism.

"When young men are labeled a threat simply because they are Arab or Muslim, . . . it is not hard to imagine the result: alienation, anger and silence."

Racial Profiling Will Make America Less Safe

David Harris

In the following viewpoint David Harris argues that racial profiling—using a person's race to help determine whether he or she is a potential criminal—is an unnecessary and ineffective tool in the fight against terrorism. He contends that labeling young men as security threats because of their appearance will worsen law enforcement and intelligence agencies' relationship with Arab and Muslim communities and make it more difficult for agents to gather vital information about potential terrorist threats. Harris further argues that the reliance on profiling may backfire if the al-Qaeda terrorist network—the organization responsible for the September 11, 2001, attacks—decides to employ terrorists who are not Middle Eastern Muslims. Harris is a professor of law at the University of Toledo and the author of *Profiles in Justice: Why Racial Profiling Cannot Work.*

As you read, consider the following questions:

1. In Harris's opinion, what is "one of the most important tools" in the fight against terrorism?
2. According to the author, what do Americans need to realize about the al-Qaeda terrorist network?
3. What is the basic test that racial profiling fails, in the author's view?

The U.S. Department of Justice's announcement that it intends to interview 3,000 more young Middle Easterners who are not suspected of criminal activity demonstrates a stubborn reliance on a crime-fighting tool that has consistently proven counterproductive: racial profiling. Indeed, despite Attorney General [John] Ashcroft's claims that the earlier effort to interview 5,000 non-immigrant men yielded "a significant number of leads," officials could point to only 20 arrests for visa violations; none with any relation to [the September 11, 2001, terrorist attacks]. Furthermore, the Attorney General's assertion that this dragnet operation improved community relations is, quite simply, ludicrous.

"Fishing Expeditions"

The collection of intelligence is one of the most important tools in the anti-terror struggle. If we are to avoid future attacks, we must gather information from those most likely to know people with ties to terrorist networks like Al Qaeda; which means that we need good, cooperative relationships with Arab and Muslim communities. By conducting broad "fishing expeditions" that round up people based on their heritage, we send a message that works counter to this objective: that we regard members of these communities not as partners, but as potential terrorists. When young men are labeled a threat simply because they are Arab or Muslim, when many are detained indefinitely on petty immigration violations, and when even some who have come forward to help have been rewarded with incarceration, it is not hard to imagine the result: alienation, anger and silence.

Thus it is not surprising that Attorney General John Ashcroft's directive ordering the "voluntary" questioning of 5,000 Middle Eastern men last November [2001] was met by skepticism in a number of police departments. Many quickly but quietly rejected the plan and told the feds to handle the questioning themselves. Command staff recognized the damage that this questioning would do to their efforts to build crime-fighting partnerships with their Middle Eastern communities. Eight former FBI officials, including former FBI and CIA chief William H. Webster, went on record to voice doubts about the law enforcement value of these tactics. One of these former officials called the wholesale questioning "the Perry Mason School of Law Enforcement" that would produce little but "the recipe to Mom's chicken soup."

A Degrading Experience

Although both President [George W.] Bush and Attorney General John Ashcroft have publicly condemned hate crimes against those who appear to be Arab, the simultaneous hyperactivity surrounding national security has sanctioned racial profiling. Passengers who appear "Arab looking," which has included those who are South Asian and Latino, have been asked to leave airplanes because both fellow passengers and crew members refuse to fly with them. Sikh men have been denied the right to even board aircraft because they refuse to fly without their turbans, something Harmeet Dhillon, co-founder of the Sikh Communications Council, equates with asking a woman to fly without her skirt. "It's humiliating and degrading," she says.

Nicole Davis, *ColorLines*, December 2001.

Indeed, senior U.S. intelligence officials circulated a memorandum early in the fall [2001] that warned about the dangers of profiling. This memorandum, first reported in the *Boston Globe*, urged law enforcement and intelligence agents against racial profiling. Profiling would fail, the memorandum said; the only way to catch terrorists was the observation of suspicious behavior. It's too bad that this warning never seems to have penetrated to the senior levels of the Department of Justice leadership.

The Risks of Profiling

Attorney General Ashcroft says that this next round of interviewees "fit the criteria of persons who might have knowledge of foreign-based terrorists." There are grave risks in this strategy; if for no other reason that it demonstrates a serious misunderstanding of Al Qaeda. The most important thing for us to realize about this organization is not that it is murderous, nor that it is made up of radical Muslims mostly from the Middle East, but that Al Qaeda has shown itself to be intelligent, patient, and thoroughly adaptable. And it is these qualities that make it a formidable enemy. The attack on the World Trade Center on September 11, was not the first but the second assault on this landmark. When the first attack, in 1993, failed to accomplish their goal, the terrorists pulled back and took eight years to devise an entirely new method of attack, plan it down to the smallest detail, and then practice it so that it could be carried out almost perfectly. This set of qualities remains very much alive in the Al Qaeda structure. In the aftermath of September 11, we began to harden cockpit doors, check carry on bags and profile Middle Eastern men. Al Qaeda's reaction was Richard Reid—a non-Arab, non–Middle Easterner from England, a British citizen with a valid U.K. passport and a bomb in his shoe. They knew what we were looking for and did not repeat what they had done in the past. A continued focus on racial profiling, whether in airports or by federal agents, threatens to blinker our vision and make it easier for our enemies to attack.

Those who insist on the "common sense" of profiling in FBI questioning and in airports want a fast food solution—something comforting for "us," that only inconveniences "them." But there is little reason to think racial profiling during the war on terrorism will be any more successful than racial profiling during the war on drugs. It is not hard to understand the impulse to take action—any action—when faced with a murderous enemy like Al Qaeda. But our actions must pass a basic test that racial profiling fails: they must help, not hinder, our efforts to fight terrorism and keep Americans safe.

"The vast majority of [immigrants are] perfectly benign, but there are indeed terrorists . . . who would use this flow of people as cover to harm us."

Immigration Must Be Restricted to Protect America Against Terrorists

Mark Krikorian

The federal government must limit the number of people it allows to enter the United States because the immigrant community poses a threat to national security, Mark Krikorian argues in the following viewpoint. According to Krikorian, immigrant enclaves, in particular Muslim communities, have given rise to terrorist cells throughout the United States. He contends that some immigrants join terrorist groups while others unwittingly aid terrorists by helping them open bank accounts and find housing. He concludes that the best way to ensure America's security is by curtailing immigration from countries that are havens for terrorists. Krikorian is the director of the Center for Immigration Studies, a think tank that studies the effects of immigration on the United States.

As you read, consider the following questions:
1. How does the author define globalization?
2. What does Krikorian consider the most disturbing example of terrorist recruitment?
3. What steps does Krikorian suggest to ensure that immigrants are loyal to America?

In 2002, there were more than 33,000,000 foreign-born residents living in the United States, approximately one-fifth of all the people worldwide living outside the country of their birth. But that's only one part of the phenomenon of population mobility. In 2001, in addition to granting permanent residence (green cards) to more than one million people, the United States also performed approximately thirty-three million inspections of foreign visitors (not immigrants) entering the United States legally through ports of entry—some of those inspections being of people who had entered more than once during that year. Add to that figure the cross-border commuters and Americans returning from abroad, and the number of border inspections conducted in 2001 surpassed 400,000,000.

American policymakers should take this amount of human traffic seriously as the security threat it is. Granted, the vast majority of this traffic is perfectly benign, but there are indeed terrorists and criminals overseas who would use this flow of people as cover to harm us. And although better technology, better intelligence, and better international cooperation are necessary, they are insufficient to make America secure from such threats. They will not do the job unless combined with reductions in the total number of people admitted to the country and changes in the criteria for the selection of those people.

There are two reasons for this, one administrative and one social. The administrative reason is that such an enormous flow of people makes it impossible for the government to devote adequate resources to keeping the bad guys out and removing those that get in. The Immigration and Naturalization Service (INS)—and the State Department, which issues visas—have been notoriously ineffective at immigration control, and it is simply not credible to claim that we can significantly reform these tools in the midst of today's very high level of arrivals from overseas. Even the move of most immigration functions to the new Department of Homeland Security, and the division of those functions between enforcement (such as border patrol and airport inspections) and services (granting green cards, citizenship status, and so forth) will not be of much help without reductions in the workload.

The Danger of Globalization

But let us suspend our disbelief for a moment and ask the deeper question, namely whether there are factors inherent in globalization that make the mass movement of people a security threat? Here we come to the social reason for reducing the movement of people into the United States.

Globalization—understood as the unfolding implications of advanced communications and transportation technologies—fosters the creation of transnational communities, which impede the kind of deep assimilation that undergirds national cohesion and fosters genuine loyalty. These poorly assimilated communities (within the United States and other countries), which globalization both creates and keeps connected to their overseas counterparts, serve as the sea within which terrorists and criminals can swim as fish, to borrow an image from [Chinese leader Mao Zedong.]

Of course, this is nothing new: immigrant communities have always been home to gangs of bad guys (though, interestingly, some research suggests that individual immigrants may be less likely than natives to be criminals). The Italian criminal organizations that cropped up in the United States early in the last century are the best-known examples, but there were prominent Jewish and Irish gangs as well. During the great wave of immigration near the turn of the twentieth century, and for more than a generation after it was stopped in the 1920s, the Mafia flourished and law enforcement had very little success penetrating it. This was because immigrants had little stake in the larger society, lived in enclaves with limited knowledge of English, were suspicious of government institutions, and clung to Old World prejudices and attitudes like "omerta" (the code of silence).

Thus it should be no surprise that similar problems exist today, with immigrant communities exhibiting characteristics that shield or even promote criminality. For instance, as criminologist Ko-lin Chin has written, "The isolation of the Chinese community, the inability of American law enforcement authorities to penetrate the Chinese criminal underworld, and the reluctance of Chinese victims to come forward for help all conspire to enable Chinese gangs to endure." In addition to the Chinese, William Kleinknecht, author of *The New Ethnic*

Mobs (1996), documents Russian, Latin American, and other criminal organizations using immigrant communities for cover and sustenance.

The greatest threat was alluded to by President [George W.] Bush in his address to the joint session of Congress after the [September 11, 2001, terrorist attacks]: "Al Qaeda is to terror what the Mafia is to crime." The role—however unwilling in most cases—of today's immigrant communities as hosts for terrorists is clear. A *New York Times* story observed about Paterson, N.J., "The hijackers' stay here also shows how, in an area that speaks many languages and keeps absorbing immigrants, a few young men with no apparent means of support and no furniture can settle in for months without drawing attention." ("A Hub for Hijackers Found in New Jersey," *New York Times*, September 27, 2001).

An Active Role in Terrorism

Nor is the role of the immigrant community always merely passive. Two of the September 11 hijackers—Nawaf Alhamzi and Khalid Almihdhar—had been embraced by the Muslim immigrant community in San Diego. As the *Washington Post* noted, "From their arrival here in late 1999 until they departed a few months before the September 11 attacks, Alhazmi and Almihdhar repeatedly enlisted help from San Diego's mosques and established members of its Islamic community. The terrorists leaned on them to find housing, open a bank account, obtain car insurance—even, at one point, get a job." ("Hijackers Found Welcome Mat on West Coast; San Diego Islamic Community Unwittingly Aided Two Who Crashed into Pentagon," *Washington Post*, December 29, 2001).

Even more threatening than the role immigrant enclaves play in simply shielding terrorists is their role in recruiting new ones. The *San Francisco Chronicle* described naturalized U.S. citizen Khalid Abu al Dahab as "a one-man communications hub" for al Qaeda, shuttling money and fake passports to terrorists around the world from his Silicon Valley apartment. According to the *Chronicle*, "Dahab said [terrorist leader Osama] bin Laden was eager to recruit American citizens of Middle Eastern descent." When Dahab and fellow terrorist and naturalized citizen Ali Mohammed (a U.S. army veteran and author of al Qaeda's terrorist handbook) traveled to Afghanistan in the mid-1990s to report on their efforts to recruit American citizens, "bin Laden praised their efforts and emphasized the necessity of recruiting as many Muslims with American citizenship as possible into the organization."

Perhaps the most disturbing example so far of such re-cruitment in immigrant communities comes from Lack-awanna, New York, where six Yemeni Americans—five of them born and raised in the United States to immigrant par-ents—were arrested in September 2002 for operating an al Qaeda terrorist sleeper cell. The alleged ringleader of the cell, also born in the United States, is believed to be hiding in Yemen. The six arrested men are accused of traveling to Pakistan . . . , ostensibly for religious training, and then go-ing to an al Qaeda terrorist training camp in Afghanistan. The community that bred this cell is made up largely of im-migrants and is intimately connected to its home country. As the *Buffalo News* put it: "This is a piece of ethnic America where the Arabic-speaking Al-Jazeera television station is beamed in from Qatar through satellite dishes to Yemenite-American homes; where young children answer 'Salaam' when the cell phone rings, while older children travel to the Middle East to meet their future husband or wife; where soccer moms don't seem to exist, and where girls don't get to play soccer or, as some would say, "football."

Nor is this likely to be the last such cell uncovered. As an-other story in the *Buffalo News* reported, "Federal officials say privately that there could be dozens of similar cells across the country, together posing a grave danger to na-tional security. They believe that such cells tend to be con-centrated in communities with large Arab populations, such as Detroit."

Assimilation Has Changed

In considering what to do about all this, the lessons of the past aren't entirely applicable. With the end of mass immi-gration, and in the absence of cheap and easy trans-Atlantic links, the assimilation of Italian immigrants in the early twentieth century accelerated, and immigrants' offspring developed a sense of genuine membership and ownership in America—what John Fonte has called "patriotic assimilation." It was this process that drained the waters within which the Mafia had been able to swim, allowing law enforcement to do its job more effectively, and eventually cripple the organizations.

Immigration Status of Foreign-Born Terrorists, 1993–2001

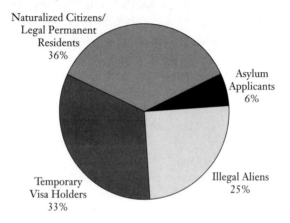

Naturalized Citizens/ Legal Permanent Residents 36%

Asylum Applicants 6%

Temporary Visa Holders 33%

Illegal Aliens 25%

Steven A. Camarota, *The Open Door*, 2002.

Thirty years ago, anthropologist Francis Ianni described this process: "An era of Italo-American crime seems to be passing in large measure due to the changing character of the Italo-American community," including "the disappearance of the kinship model on which such [Mafia] families are based." Ianni continued, "After three generations of acculturation," Ianni continued, "this powerful pattern of organization is finally losing its hold on Italo-Americans generally—and on the crime families as well." Kleinknecht, in *The New Ethnic Mobs*, argues that the same could happen today in other immigrant communities: "If the mass immigration of Chinese should come to a halt, the Chinese gangster may disappear in a blaze of assimilation after a couple of decades."

Maybe, but globalization has changed the terms of assimilation, making such an outcome much more difficult. In the

138

past, it was all but impossible to live in two countries simultaneously, which forced most newcomers to put down permanent roots. Of course, immigrants in the past tried to maintain ties with the old country, but the cost and difficulties involved were such that the ties tended to atrophy fairly quickly. As Princeton sociologist Alejandro Portes observes, "Earlier in the twentieth century, the expense and difficulty of long-distance communication and travel simply made it impossible to lead a dual existence in two countries. Polish peasants couldn't just hop a plane or make a phone call, for that matter, to check out how things were going at home over the weekend."

But now, with low-cost long-distance rates and air fares, a transnational life is available to the masses. Wellesley sociologist Peggy Levitt has even described what she calls a "transnational village," a community split between the original village in the Dominican Republic and its doppelganger in Boston. Political parties operate in both places, people watch the same soap operas, telephone contacts become ever more frequent as rates fall, gossip travels instantly between the two halves of the village, parents in one half try to raise children in the other.

Another notable example is Jesus R. Galvis, a Colombian immigrant who started a business in New Jersey, became an American citizen, and eventually got elected to the Hackensack City Council (He's still there). In 1998, he ran for the Senate—the Colombian Senate. Had he won, he would have held elective office in two nations simultaneously, a first in American history. In 2000, at least three Mexican immigrants living in the United States ran for local political offices in Mexico, a phenomenon likely to proliferate wildly in the wake of Mexico's passage of a law permitting dual nationality and the fact that within the next few years immigrants living in the U.S. will be able to vote in Mexican elections.

The Disunited States

This process, repeated all across America by immigrants from many different countries, is blurring the distinction between immigrants and sojourners. As such, it is aiding the transformation of the United States from a unified nation, which admitted immigrants in order to make them full members of the national community, into merely "one node in a post-national network of diasporas," in the words of University of Chicago anthropologist Arjun Appadurai.

The effects of this "network of diasporas" trend in globalization is evident in recent research done on national self-identification. The aforementioned Professor Portes, with Ruben Rumbaut of Michigan State, recently published *Legacies: The Story of the Immigrant Second Generation* (2001), the product of a multi-year longitudinal study of thousands of children of immigrants in San Diego and South Florida. Most interesting for our purposes was their analysis of how these young people identified their nationality, something they were asked when they started high school and again when they were finishing.

When first surveyed, the majority of the students identified themselves as Americans in some form, either as simply "American" or as a hyphenated American (Cuban-American, for instance, or Filipino-American). After four years of American high school, barely one-third still identified themselves in this way; the majority choosing an identification with no American component at all, opting for either a foreign national-origin identity (Cuban, Filipino) or a racial identity (Hispanic, Asian).

A rare study of the identifications of Muslim immigrants wasn't any more reassuring. Kambiz Ghanea Bassiri, an Iranian doctoral student at Harvard, found that the Muslim immigrants he surveyed were at least more likely to feel "closer ties or loyalties" to Islamic countries than to the United States. Similarly, the 2002 (U.S.) National Survey of Latinos, released in December [2002] by the Pew Hispanic Center, found that even among the grandchildren of Hispanic immigrants, only 57 percent thought of themselves as primarily American.

Ending Radical Multiculturalism

What to do? The solutions already undertaken, though insufficient, are a first step. Better identification systems, greater scrutiny of money transfers, more attention by intelligence and law-enforcement agencies to penetrating terrorist and criminal groups are all necessary measures. In addition, there are steps we can take to better ensure that those who move to our society learn to love America, comfort her, honor and keep her, in sickness and in health, forsaking all others, as long as they live. Improved American history education, as championed by President Bush, is a must, as are efforts to raise the standards for naturalization and curb radical multiculturalism.

Ultimately, however, America's security in a globalized world depends on the curtailment of the mass admission of people, especially from less-developed societies where terrorist and criminal organizations are more likely to flourish.

*"For all its potential pitfalls, multiculturalism
actually strengthens U.S. national security."*

Immigrants Enhance National Security

Daniel Smith

In the following viewpoint Daniel Smith asserts that America's multicultural makeup—the result of two centuries of immigration—has not harmed national security or increased the likelihood of terrorist attacks. On the contrary, he argues that multiculturalism has improved national security, as illustrated during World War II when a regiment of Japanese Americans was recognized as the best U.S. assault troop in the European theater. In fact, he maintains, immigrants should be valued precisely because they can better understand the threats posed by their countries of origin and help Americans avoid terrorist attacks. He concludes that rather than feel threatened by immigrants, Americans should look to multiculturalism as an important component of national defense. Smith is the chief of research at the Center for Defense Information, a nonpartisan organization that analyzes America's defense.

As you read, consider the following questions:
1. In Smith's view, what can fear of "them" lead to?
2. How did James Madison define "faction," as quoted by Smith?
3. What is the greatest strength of the United States, in the author's opinion?

[The September 11, 2001, terrorist attacks have] rekindled in some Americans prejudices, suspicions and a wariness of "them" as opposed to "us." Many who now look askance at certain ethnic or religious groups confess that their reactions are almost involuntary, knee-jerk responses to descriptions of the perpetrators of the attacks.

We are witnessing the effects of a primordial animal emotion: fear. But the insecurity gripping the nation today does not result in fight or flight so much as it does finger-pointing. Compounding the problem is the fact that the Bush administration has sent mixed messages about "them" which in turn has rekindled an old fear: that a different culture is a threat to national security.

To his credit President George W. Bush has been determined to dissociate the religion of the 19 perpetrators as a motivating force for their actions by branding their interpretation of Islam as extremist. Conversely, most of the individuals questioned or being held by the Justice Department are of "Middle Eastern" origin, and most of the financial assets the administration wants to freeze are of organizations and individuals based in that region.

A Corrosive Fear

In a country that was created from and has thrived on the contributions of many cultures, fear of "them" is highly corrosive. It induces hate crimes and breeds distrust; it can lead to a diminution of rights and civil liberties as insecure, citizens demand their government take action in the name of national security. In such an atmosphere, "multiculturalism" takes a beating. But it deserves better. For all its potential pitfalls, multiculturalism actually strengthens U.S. national security.

Before going further, it might be helpful to describe what is meant by "culture." At root, culture is a type of shared experience, "a distinct complex of tradition of a racial, religious or social group" that includes "knowledge, belief, morals, law, customs, opinions, religion, superstition and art," all of which are susceptible to being transmitted from generation to generation through language, artifact and example.

More importantly, culture is malleable. Like any message transmitted among a number of people, culture changes over time. It is affected by discoveries, education, innovations and contacts with other cultures. And where two or more cultures meet, the ensuing relationship either can be a blending that creates a hybrid (as in the United States) or a clash (as in Samuel Huntington's phrase, "the clash of civilizations") in which each seeks to dominate the other(s).

For most of human history, the blending of distinctly different peoples has lost out to conflict. The fear of losing control over one's future kept "we" and "them" at swords' point. Modern political clashes have amplified the divisive effects of multiculturalism; these fissures have provoked jeremiads from cultural purists urging a return to the golden age—usually a mythic period in which "their" culture dominated.

The Rise of Nationalism

While the 1648 Peace of Westphalia[1] laid the foundation for the modern European system of nation-states, it could be argued that the conscious cultivation of nationalism in the late 18th and early 19th centuries was the emotional engine that powered the drive for greater uniformity within states. In this emotionally charged context, each regime's worst fear was of a religious or ethnic "fifth column" intent on betraying the state to its enemies. Ethnic minorities became most suspect, particularly if in a neighboring country they were a majority.

Even the great émigré destinations of Australia, Canada and the United States did not fully escape this mind-set. But their expansive territory and social mobility tended to mitigate the effects of intolerance. Moreover, each succeeding wave of immigrants, regardless of their origin, shared similar hopes, fears, expectations and experiences with those who had arrived before them. Most significantly, the motivation of émigrés— to find freedom to choose their own way in the world, to be in control of their destinies and thus be secure—bound them to an idea that transcended all cultures. They understood that their individual security was linked to the national security of their adopted country. Indeed, belief in democracy and human rights for all became the American culture.

Those who indict multiculturalism as a threat to national

1. the treaty that ended the Thirty Years' War

security seem to equate culture with faction, as James Madison understood the term. In *Federalist No. 10*, Madison defined faction as "a number of citizens, whether amounting to a majority or a minority of the whole, who are united and actuated by some common impulse of passion, or of interest, adverse to the rights of other citizens, or to the permanent and aggregate interests of the community." He then says one way to remove the causes of faction is "by giving to every citizen the same opinions, the same passions and the same interests."

It is true that cultural enclaves developed in big cities and defined rural areas, many of which persist to this day. But in holding to their customs and lifestyles, the members of these communities do not attempt to deny the rights and freedoms of others. They treasure these rights and freedoms, demonstrating every day "the same passions and the same interests" as their fellow citizens.

In fact, during the 20th century it was the majority, not scattered cultural minorities, that became an impassioned faction. In World War I, those of German ancestry came under suspicion, so much so that many Anglicized their surnames. In World War II, those of Japanese ancestry, even U.S. citizens, were subject to detention and internment. Now, at the start of the 21st century, this pattern is re-emerging. But as in the 20th century, it remains shortsighted.

Multiculturalism Enhances Security

The logic of ensuring national security in a multicultural world demands a multicultural approach. Who better can understand an enemy's motivations and psychology than a person who has shared the same cultural experiences? Who better to act as an interpreter or to interrogate prisoners of war, defectors or line-crossers than a native speaker who understands idioms and linguistic innuendos? During international discussions affecting national security, who better to advise negotiators than one whose life experiences are rooted in the culture of the other side?

The U.S. military history of World War II illustrates the contributions of multiculturalism to our nation's security. One of the most famous U.S. Army units in the European theater arguably was the 442nd Regimental Combat Team

(RCT). It was composed entirely of Nisei, citizens of Japanese-American descent. In 20 months and eight major campaigns, the regiment won seven Presidential Unit Citations and more than 18,100 personal decorations, and came to be regarded as the best U.S. assault troops in the theater.

The unstinting performance of the 442nd's members was particularly remarkable because they had an additional burden to that of other soldiers. Many of their families were in internment camps and, in light of their heritage, their loyalty was suspect and their liberties under a cloud. But they were solidly "Americans first."

The End of the INS

Effective March 1, 2003, the Immigration and Naturalization Service (INS) was dissolved, and the enforcement and services functions of that troubled agency were transferred to the new Department of Homeland Security (DHS). Although the INS is only one of 22 federal agencies and departments that will be folded into DHS, the transfer of immigration functions to a department that provides frontline defense against terrorism in the United States likely will have profound implications for how the country views—and treats—immigrants. As one commentator suggested, "Placing all of INS's functions into a department focused primarily on national security suggests that the United States no longer views immigrants as welcome contributors, but as potential threats viewed through a terrorist lens."

Lawyers Committee for Human Rights, *Imbalance of Powers*, 2003.

In the Pacific, American Indians known as the Navaho Code Talkers participated in every assault landing by U.S. Marines from 1942 to the war's end. They were in all major Marine units transmitting messages by telephone and radio in their native language—a code that the Japanese never broke. Their native tongue, a unique cultural "artifact" was the perfect encryption system because no Japanese understood the Navaho language. (Actually, American Indian languages had been used on a less-expansive scale in World War I to encrypt messages before transmission.)

Perhaps more surprising, given the war's internment policies, was the presence of some 6,000 ethnic Japanese in the

Pacific theater in various military-intelligence organizations. They, like the Code Talkers, saw action as linguists in every campaign from New Guinea to Okinawa. But World War II was a "traditional" or conventional war, with defined battle lines and armies that contested along fronts stretching in some cases for thousands of kilometers. What about wars where there are no continuous front lines, where "the front" is a 360-degree circle that marks a unit's perimeter? What about "fourth-generation warfare" where the front appears and disappears as forces rapidly mass, attack and then disperse? Or the ultimate in modern unconventional warfare: a small group of determined fanatics, supported by cells woven into society's fabric, that unexpectedly strikes using unanticipated means (the September 11 scenario)?

Taking Advantage of Diversity

The problems and failures are not with multiculturalism. They are in not deploying the resources that multiculturalism affords. The warning signs for September 11 were evident a decade ago when Algerian terrorists hijacked an Air France jet, intending to crash it into the Eiffel Tower. Failure to anticipate what one's enemies might do reveals a lack of understanding of their psychology. Even under the best of circumstances, a foreign psychology is difficult to fathom; it can be nearly impossible for those who merely have studied a culture or had cursory experience of it. If there is a weakness to be corrected, it is the screening and evaluation of individuals—but not as cultural "representatives"—as they seek to enter the country. Again, for those concerned with national security a multicultural society, if it properly employs this diversity, provides the best defense against the entry of those wishing to destroy, not build, society.

The diversity of the United States is its greatest strength; it produces a synthesis that is more than the sum of its parts. The "clash of civilizations" through the give-and-take of ideas, produces innovations that are prized in a myriad of professions such as business and finance (both aspects of national security), as well as the military. It also produces respect for the rights of all.

Our internal and diplomatic history demonstrates that security for one faction, group or nation is impossible if it means insecurity for others. In the 21st century, as transnational forces become stronger and as communications and travel become more rapid, it is more imperative for governments to recognize that national security now is a function of international security. In such a world, multiculturalism is our first line of offense and defense.

Periodical Bibliography

The following articles have been selected to supplement the diverse views presented in this chapter.

Rob Ashgar	"A Show of Grace for Safety's Sake," *Los Angeles Times*, July 6, 2002.
Jerry Berman et al.	"Guarding the Home Front," *Reason*, December 2001.
Matthew Brzezinski	"Fortress America," *New York Times Magazine*, February 23, 2003.
Nicole Davis	"The Slippery Slope of Racial Profiling," *ColorLines*, December 2001.
Valerie L. Demmer	"Civil Liberties and Homeland Security," *Humanist*, January/February 2002.
Ekaterina Drozdova and Michael Samoilov	"Security *and* Liberty," *Hoover Digest*, Winter 2002.
Amitai Etzioni	"Better Safe than Sorry," *Weekly Standard*, July 21, 2003.
William Norman Grigg	"From Law to Lawlessness," *New American*, October 7, 2002.
Nat Hentoff	"Ashcroft vs. the Constitution," *Free Inquiry*, Winter 2002/2003.
Scott Johnson	"Better Unsafe than (Occasionally) Sorry?" *American Enterprise*, January/February 2003.
Wendy Kaminer	"Fear vs. Freedom," *UU World*, January/February 2003.
Charles Lane	"Fighting Terror vs. Defending Liberties," *Washington Post National Weekly Edition*, September 9–15, 2002.
Damien Lawson	"Refugee! Terrorist! Criminal!" *New Internationalist*, October 2002.
Heather MacDonald	"Total Misrepresentation," *Weekly Standard*, January 27, 2003.
Laurence H. Tribe	"We Can Strike a Balance on Civil Liberties," *Wall Street Journal*, September 27, 2001.

CHAPTER 4

How Should the International Community Respond to Terrorism?

Chapter Preface

The first few years of the twenty-first century have been marked by the never-ending threat of terrorism. As terrorist acts leave people throughout the world feeling vulnerable and fearful, many have begun to wonder if the international community should use torture to extract confessions and information from suspected terrorists to thwart future terrorist attacks.

Although the UN Geneva Convention Against Torture prohibits all types of torture, the practice has been used against terrorist suspects, including in Israel, which has since disallowed such procedures, and Great Britain. Physical torture has traditionally been forbidden in the United States on the grounds that it violates the constitutional ban on "cruel and unusual punishment." Despite this official ban, the United States has not been immune from charges that it uses less-than-savory methods when questioning suspects. For example, Amnesty International has criticized U.S. officials for authorizing interrogation methods against Khalid Shaikh Mohammed—one of the men believed to have orchestrated the September 11, 2001, terrorist attacks—that the human rights organization believes too closely resembles torture. In particular Amnesty International is critical of the use of shackling, denial of medical care, and hooding. The White House has denied the charges and asserted that Mohammed was being treated properly under international law.

Not everyone agrees that torture should be banned. In his book *Why Terrorism Works*, lawyer Alan M. Dershowitz evaluates the pros and cons of torturing terrorist suspects. He notes that although torture does not always thwart terrorist plots, the fact that it is sometimes successful explains why it is still in use. Dershowitz asserts that using nonlethal torture—for example, inserting a sterilized needle under a suspect's fingernails—in order to thwart a terrorist attack that could kill thousands of people can be justified. He writes, "Pain is a lesser and more remediable harm than death; and the lives of a thousand innocent people should be valued more than the bodily integrity of one guilty person." However, Dershowitz cautions that permitting torture under limited circumstances could result in a slippery slope, where countries turn to increasingly brutal forms of torture in order to save fewer and fewer people. He concludes that the best way to ensure that governments do not misuse torture is to establish strict standards for its use.

As terrorism is a global problem, the international community must work together to find a way to prevent future attacks. The authors in the following chapter consider several global responses to terrorism.

> *"The United Nations [is] the one truly international body that exists for the purpose of dealing with an international crime."*

The United Nations Should Lead the Fight Against Terrorism

Alexa McDonough

In the following viewpoint Alexa McDonough, former leader of Canada's New Democratic Party, asserts that efforts to end terrorism must be led by the United Nations. She contends that the UN is best suited to respond to terror because it can establish an international tribunal that would indict and convict the people behind the September 11, 2001, terrorist attacks. According to McDonough international justice must be chosen over military retaliation because no country, or coalition of countries, should be permitted to take the law into its own hands when fighting terrorism.

As you read, consider the following questions:

1. According to the author, what previous crises prompted the UN to establish international courts?
2. In McDonough's view, why should no coalition or country be permitted to "take the law into its own hands"?
3. What should Canadians not accept, according to McDonough?

Alexa McDonough, "Let UN Bring Terrorists to Justice," *Canadian Speeches*, September/October 2001.

The [New Democratic Party] opposes the U.S.-led military coalition and Canada's participation in it.[1] Terrorism must be suppressed and the perpetrators of the September 11 [2001] atrocities must be brought to justice, by force if necessary. But no nation or coalition of nations should be judge, jury and executioner. The job must be done under the auspices of the United Nations.

Let us also be clear that the atrocities committed on September 11 were indeed a crime, a horrendous crime, a crime against humanity. It is very important that we be clear about that because that fact must guide us in our response to the atrocities of September 11. We know that when we are dealing with crimes a response to criminality is required and that we must use every single means at our disposal around the world to bring the perpetrators of these horrendous crimes to justice.

Seeking an International Response

The terrorism of September 11 is also a terrorism that is now recognized as a global crisis, so our response to these crimes must also be a truly international response.

As people understand the implication of what we are faced with, the number of voices is growing as people call for a response based upon the rule of law which is truly international, understanding that we are dealing with crimes against humanity. That is why we have consistently advocated and argued for a special international court to be established under the auspices of the United Nations, similar to those that have been set up to deal with the horrors of what happened in Rwanda, in the former Yugoslavia, and in the Lockerbie bombing.[2]

Those situations are not all the same, but the mechanism, the moral and legal authority to deal with these crimes

1. This refers to the decision to go to war against Afghanistan and its government, the Taliban, which had links to the terrorists behind the September 11, 2001, attacks. 2. Between April and June 1994, an estimated 800,000 Rwandans were massacred following the assassination of Rwandan president Juvenal Habyarimana. Habyarimana was a member of the Hutu ethnic group; most of the people who committed the murders were Hutus, with the majority of victims from the other predominant ethnic group, the Tutsis. Civil war in Yugoslavia led to ethnic cleansing during the 1990s. On December 21, 1988, Pan Am Flight 103 was blown out of the sky above Lockerbie, Scotland; 270 people died.

against humanity that are literally a global crisis, must reside with the United Nations, the one truly international body that exists for the purpose of dealing with an international crime and dealing with the kind of threat to peace and security around the world that is reflected in what happened on September 11.

A Vital Role

The United Nations, as a global organization, has a vital role to play in channelling the international outrage with terrorist attacks and resolve in combating terrorism into a sound, coordinated multifaceted strategy, which includes legal conventions, cooperation between States and their law enforcement agencies, sharing of information and intelligence, and developing and implementing mechanisms to suppress financial support to terrorist groups, etc.

Pino Arlacchi, *UN Chronicle*, September–November, 2001.

What would such an international tribunal do? Such an international tribunal would do what we do when faced with horrendous crimes. It would indict. It would apprehend. It would try and it would punish the perpetrators of those horrendous crimes.

Not a One-Nation Fight

To decide to give any nation or any coalition of countries, no matter how broad, the right to act as judge, jury and executioner when dealing with horrendous crimes is simply not acceptable. No country or coalition can take the law into its own hands, because if we allow that to happen we descend into lawlessness and the implications for the future peace and security of the world are truly terrifying.

Let me be clear: I am not among the fainthearted and my party is not naive. The use of force may indeed be necessary to bring those perpetrators to justice, but let us make sure that the moral and legal authority for acting to bring them to justice, including if necessary the use of force, is carried out within the rule of law and under the auspices of the United Nations.

We simply cannot choose retaliation and military strikes

over international justice and many people with far more experience in the realm of international law, international relations, and international diplomacy have pleaded this case. Let me quote one. Geoffrey Pearson, a distinguished diplomat, son of a distinguished prime minister who knew and understood this argument, and today the president of the United Nations Association in Canada, cautions that "such action will only escalate the cycle of violence and is likely to create a new [generation] blighted by hatred and despair."

Do Not Blame the United States

Canadians were profoundly horrified by the [three thousand] senseless deaths in the United States on September 11. We simply cannot remain indifferent to the deaths of more innocent people, to the deaths of more men, women and children in some other part of the world. Nor clearly can we accept, and I want to be very clear about this, that the horrendous crimes of September 11 are in any way, shape or form justifiable. There is no cause and no grievance sufficient to justify the crimes against humanity that happened on September 11. That is why the New Democratic Party has been very clear about distancing itself from any who would argue that somehow the past wrongs of one nation, in this case the United States of America, would explain and justify the September 11 atrocities. They do not, they cannot, and they never will.

Just as all nations of the world must come together under the auspices of the United Nations with moral and legal authority that only that body alone lends to this fight against terrorism, it is also absolutely essential that the United Nations takes the lead in the campaign against terrorism, and it is doing just that.

"We are faced with the sordid spectacle of globalist insiders . . . exploiting war and tragedy to further empower the United Nations."

The United Nations Should Not Lead the Fight Against Terrorism

Steve Bonta

In the following viewpoint Steve Bonta maintains that the United States should not allow the United Nations to lead the fight against terrorism. He argues that although the UN presents itself as being able to establish a broad coalition of states that is better suited than a single nation to quell global terror, its true goals are far different. In Bonta's opinion, the organization is more interested in using the September 11, 2001, terrorist attacks and the subsequent war in Afghanistan (where the hijackers were purportedly trained) to destroy American sovereignty and trick Americans into surrendering their constitutional freedoms to unaccountable international agencies. Bonta is a contributing editor to the *New American* magazine.

As you read, consider the following questions:
1. In the author's view how is the war in Afghanistan similar to earlier conflicts?
2. What did UN legal expert David Donalcattin say was the "great news" of the September 11, 2001, attacks, according to Bonta?
3. According to the author, who gives the federal government the right to defend the United States?

Steve Bonta, "Empowering the UN," *The New American*, vol. 17, November 5, 2001. Copyright © 2001 by American Opinion Publishing Incorporated. Reproduced by permission.

A nd now the war. With bombs and missiles falling in Afghanistan, a defiant Osama bin Laden[1] is promising that
"neither America nor the people who live in it will dream of
security before [Muslims] live it in Palestine, and not before
all the infidel armies leave the land of Muhammad." Secretary
of Defense Donald H. Rumsfeld predicted in a recent *New
York Times* editorial that this [war against terrorism] will be

> a war like none other our nation has faced. . . . It will involve
> floating coalitions of countries, which may change and
> evolve. . . . This is not a war against an individual, a group, a
> religion or a country. Rather, our opponent is a global net-
> work of terrorist organizations and their state sponsors. . . .
> Forget about "exit strategies"; we're looking at a sustained
> engagement that carries no deadlines.

So far, however, America's first war of the new century
very much resembles many of the conflicts of the last century: hi-tech missiles, warplanes, and naval task forces raining
destruction from beyond the range of obsolete air-defense
systems; raging mobs reacting to inflammatory rhetoric; and
the ominous prospect—as Secretary Rumsfeld implied—of
military engagement without any end in sight. In common
with America's post–World War II 20th-century wars—from
Korea and Vietnam to the Persian Gulf, the Balkans, Soma-
lia, and a galaxy of lesser conflicts—this one was embarked
upon without a congressional declaration of war. But unlike
any of the others, it is in response to an attack against U.S.
citizens on American soil. Terrorism, we have learned, is a legitimate threat to the security of the United States.

The True Aims of the War

But the war on terrorism—like the aforementioned 20th
century conflicts—has other aims besides the publicly stated
eradication of international terrorism. The winds of war
carry the smell of opportunity for the world's power elites.
British Prime Minister Tony Blair, in a speech to the Labor
Party, indicated that:

> Round the world, September 11th [2001] is bringing gov-

---

1. Osama bin Laden orchestrated the September 11, 2001, terrorist attacks. His
terrorist network was based in Afghanistan and supported by its government,
prompting the United States to go to war against Afghanistan in fall 2001.

ernments and people to reflect, consider and change. There is a coming together. . . . The issue is not how to stop globalisation. The issue is how we use the power of community to combine it with justice. . . . This is a moment to seize. The kaleidoscope has been shaken. The pieces are in flux. Soon they will settle again. But before they do, let us re-order this world around us.

UN Secretary-General Kofi Annan, speaking to the UN General Assembly on October [2, 2001] said of the war on terrorism:

In this struggle, there is simply no alternative to international cooperation. Terrorism will be defeated if the international community summons the will to unite in a broad coalition, or it will not be defeated at all. The United Nations is uniquely positioned to serve as the forum for this coalition. . . . The urgent business of the United Nations must now be to develop a long-term strategy, in order to ensure global legitimacy for the struggle ahead. The legitimacy that the United Nations conveys can ensure that the greatest number of states are able and willing to take the necessary and difficult steps—diplomatic, legal, and political—that are needed to defeat terrorism.

According to a September 26 [2001] article in the *Washington Times*, David Donalcattin, a UN legal expert working to set up the International Criminal Court, exulted that "the bombing, and subsequent calls for a global alliance against terrorism, has shaken Washington off its anti-multilateral course. . . . The great news for us [is] that American isolationism is finished. . . . This attack has shown, and the White House seems to hear, that no nation can do it alone."

Capitalizing on a Crisis

In other words, once again we are faced with the sordid spectacle of globalist insiders, at home and abroad, exploiting war and tragedy to further empower the United Nations. Make no mistake about it: Globalists intend to turn this conflict into yet another referendum on American sovereignty, and to gull Americans, caught in the emotion of the moment, into surrendering more of their freedom to unconstitutional and unaccountable international enforcement organs. The UN, meanwhile, emboldened by its newfound, Establishment-promoted aura of respectability and legitimacy, is poised to exact dangerous new concessions on national sovereignty from member nations.

Terror in the United Nations

[The UN Human Rights Commission] is infested with documented state sponsors of terror and human rights abusers—who will do anything to distract attention from the deadly games they play. Anyone want to venture a guess as to why so many Human Rights Commission experts are "deeply concerned" about new [U.S.] anti-terrorism measures and national security laws? The club includes such distinguished members as China, Cuba, Libya, Saudi Arabia, Sudan, Syria, and Vietnam.

Evidence contained in human rights reports produced by Freedom House . . . and the U.S. Department of State reveals that 84 UN member states are documented human rights abusers.

Fred Gedrich, "Bogus UN Human Rights Operation Seeks to Protect Terrorists," FreedomAlliance.com, January 25, 2002.

The United Nations wasted little time positioning itself at the head of the fray. The day after the attacks, the Security Council rushed out Resolution 1368, which called on states to "work together urgently to bring to justice the perpetrators, organizers, and sponsors of these attacks" and expressed "readiness to take all necessary steps to respond to the terrorist attacks of 11 September 2001, and to combat all forms of terrorism, in accordance with its responsibilities under the Charter of the United Nations." Still, Secretary of State Colin Powell, as reported by Nicholas Kralev of the *Washington Times*, said on September 26 [2001] that the United States didn't require UN approval before responding militarily to the attacks: "At the moment, notwithstanding all the coalition building we have been doing, President [George W.] Bush retains the authority to take whatever actions he believes are appropriate in accordance with the needs for self-defense of the United States and of the American people." So far so good; but Secretary Powell then added, according to Kralev, that "that authority . . . is based on Article 51 of the U.N. Charter, which gives member states the right to self-defense." In fact, the right of the federal government to defend our nation comes not from the United Nations but from U.S. citizens who have delegated that authority to the federal government via the U.S. Constitution. "We the people of the United States" established this Constitution expressly to, among other things, "provide for the common defense." In particular, the Constitution grants Congress the power "To declare war"; "To raise and support armies"; "To provide and maintain a navy"; and "To . . . repel invasions. . . ." It also, of course, makes the President "commander in chief of the Army and Navy of the United States. . . ." Surely this most basic knowledge of the U.S. system of government is not unknown to our Secretary of State?

Despite the Bush administration's unmistakable toadying to United Nations authority from the earliest stages of the crisis, the UN-based internationalist Establishment does not intend to be perceived as a mere rubber-stamp for American and British policymakers. University of Pennsylvania scholar Robert Wright, writing in the *New York Times* on September 24th [2001], touted international agreements like the Chemical Weapons Convention and the Comprehensive Test Ban Treaty as "tame" precedents for more restrictive international arms treaties to come. Wright also decried "the extreme devotion of the conservatives to national sovereignty." Changes to come, he warned, could include "the creation of international policing mechanisms that could impinge on national sovereignty as never before. . . . Clinging to American sovereignty at all costs isn't just wrong. It's impossible. . . . So the question isn't whether to surrender national sovereignty. The question is how—carefully and systematically, or chaotically and catastrophically? Get the message? The time to empower the UN and associated international organs is now, before the furor over terrorism subsides and the UN-as-world-savior message loses its appeal.

> *"There are times when waging war is not only morally permitted, but morally necessary."*

War Is an Appropriate Response to Terrorism

Enola Aird et al.

Military action against terrorists is necessary and justifiable, Enola Aird, the director of the Motherhood Project, and her fellow authors argue in the following viewpoint. They contend that war can be just if it is fought by a legitimate authority under certain restrictions, such as protecting innocents from certain harm and only targeting combatants. The authors assert that the September 11, 2001, terrorist attacks were unlawful and wanton acts justifying a military response by the United States. They conclude that war may be the best way to prevent terrorists from wreaking horrific devastation on the world. This viewpoint was issued as a letter on February 12, 2002, by the nonpartisan think tank Institute for American Values.

As you read, consider the following questions:
1. What is sometimes the first and most important reply to evil, according to the authors?
2. In the authors' view, what type of violence is never morally acceptable?
3. How has Islam argued against violent atrocities, according to Aird et al.?

Enola Aird et al., "What We're Fighting For: A Letter from America," *Responsive Community*, vol. 12, Fall 2002, p. 30. Copyright © 2002 by the Institute of American Values. Reproduced by permission.

At times, it becomes necessary for a nation to defend itself through force of arms. Because war is a grave matter, involving the sacrifice and taking of precious human life, conscience demands that those who would wage the war state clearly the moral reasoning behind their actions, in order to make plain to one another, and to the world community, the principles they are defending.

We affirm five fundamental truths that pertain to all people without distinction:

1. All human beings are born free and equal in dignity and rights.
2. The basic subject of society is the human person, and the legitimate role of government is to protect and help to foster the conditions for human flourishing.
3. Human beings naturally desire to seek the truth about life's purpose and ultimate ends.
4. Freedom of conscience and religious freedom are inviolable rights of the human person.
5. Killing in the name of God is contrary to faith in God and is the greatest betrayal of the universality of religious faith.

We fight to defend ourselves and to defend these universal principles. . . .

Justifying War

We recognize that all war is terrible, representative finally of human political failure. We also know that the line separating good and evil does not run between one society and another, much less between one religion and another; ultimately, that line runs through the middle of every human heart. Finally, those of us—Jews, Christians, Muslims, and others—who are people of faith recognize our responsibility, stated in our holy scriptures, to love mercy and to do all in our power to prevent war and live in peace.

Yet reason and careful moral reflection also teach us that there are times when the first and most important reply to evil is to stop it. There are times when waging war is not only morally permitted, but morally necessary, as a response to calamitous acts of violence, hatred, and injustice. This is one of those times.

The idea of a "just war" is broadly based, with roots in many of the world's diverse religious and secular moral traditions. Jewish, Christian, and Muslim teachings, for example, all contain serious reflections on the definition of a just war. To be sure, some people, often in the name of realism, insist that war is essentially a realm of self-interest and necessity, making most attempts at moral analysis irrelevant. We disagree. Moral inarticulacy in the face of war is itself a moral stance—one that rejects the possibility of reason, accepts normlessness in international affairs, and capitulates to cynicism. To seek to apply objective moral reasoning to war is to defend the possibility of civil society and a world community based on justice.

The principles of just war teach us that wars of aggression and aggrandizement are never acceptable. Wars may not legitimately be fought for national glory, to avenge past wrongs, for territorial gain, or for any other non-defensive purpose.

The primary moral justification for war is to protect the innocent from certain harm. [Philosopher and theologian] Augustine, whose early-fifth-century book, *The City of God*, is a seminal contribution to just war thinking, argues (echoing Socrates) that it is better for the Christian as an individual to suffer harm rather than to commit it. But is the morally responsible person also required, or even permitted, to make for *other* innocent persons a commitment to non-self-defense? For Augustine, and for the broader just war tradition, the answer is no. If one has compelling evidence that innocent people who are in no position to protect themselves will be grievously harmed unless coercive force is used to stop an aggressor, then the moral principle of love of neighbor calls us to the use of force.

Legitimate Targets

Wars may not legitimately be fought against dangers that are small, questionable, or of uncertain consequence, or against dangers that might plausibly be mitigated solely through negotiation, appeals to reason, persuasion from third parties, or other nonviolent means. But if the danger to innocent life is real and certain, and especially if the aggressor is motivated by implacable hostility—if the end he seeks is not your willingness to negotiate or comply, but rather your destruction—then a resort to proportionate force is morally justified.

A just war can only be fought by a legitimate authority with responsibility for public order. Violence that is freelance, opportunistic, or individualistic is never morally acceptable.

A just war can only be waged against persons who are combatants. Just war authorities from across history and around the world—whether they be Muslim, Jewish, Christian, from other faith traditions, or secular—consistently teach us that noncombatants are immune from deliberate attack. Thus, killing civilians for revenge, or even as a means of deterring aggression from people who sympathize with them, is morally wrong. Although in some circumstances, and within strict limits, it can be morally justifiable to undertake military actions that may result in the unintended but foreseeable death or injury of some noncombatants, it is not morally acceptable to make the killing of noncombatants the operational objective of a military action.

These and other just war principles teach us that, whenever human beings contemplate or wage war, it is both possible and necessary to affirm the sanctity of human life and embrace the principle of equal human dignity. These principles strive to preserve and reflect, even in the tragic activity of war, the fundamental moral truth that "others"—those who are strangers to us, those who differ from us in race or language, those whose religions we may believe to be untrue—have the same right to life that we do, and the same human dignity and human rights that we do.

The Threat of Islamicism

On September 11, 2001, a group of individuals deliberately attacked the United States, using hijacked airplanes as weapons with which to kill, in less than two hours, over 3,000 of our citizens in New York City, southwestern Pennsylvania, and Washington, DC. Overwhelmingly, those who died on September 11 were civilians, not combatants, and were not known at all, except as Americans, by those who killed them. Those who died on the morning of September 11 were killed unlawfully, wantonly, and with premeditated malice—a kind of killing that, in the name of precision, can only be described as murder. Those murdered included people from all races, many ethnicities, most major religions. They included dishwashers and corporate executives.

American Views on War

"All in all, how should the U.S. determine its policy with regard to the war on terrorism? Should it be based mostly on the national interests of the U.S., or should it strongly take into account the interests of its allies?"

	%
U.S. interests	45
Allies' interests	35
Both	10
Neither	1
Don't know	9

"How do you see the U.S. led war on terrorism? Do you think the U.S. is taking into account the interests of its allies in the fight against terrorism, or do you think the U.S. is acting mainly on its own interests?"

	%
Allies' interests	44
U.S. interests	42
Don't know	14

"In the long run, what is the best way for the U.S. to avoid problems like terrorism? Should the U.S. be very much involved in solving international problems, or not get too involved with international problems?"

	8/02	10/01
	%	%
Very much involved	53	61
Not too involved	34	32
Don't know	13	7

Pew Research Center survey, taken between August 14 and 25, 2002.

The individuals who committed these acts of war did not act alone, or without support, or for unknown reasons. They were members of an international Islamicist network, active in as many as 40 countries, now known to the world as Al Qaeda. This group, in turn, constitutes but one arm of a larger radical Islamicist movement, growing for decades and in some instances tolerated and even supported by governments, that openly professes its desire and increasingly demonstrates its ability to use murder to advance its objectives.

We use the terms "Islam" and "Islamic" to refer to one of the world's great religions, with about 1.2 billion adherents, including several million U.S. citizens, some of whom were murdered on September 11. It ought to go without saying—but we say it here once, clearly—that the great majority of the world's Muslims, guided in large measure by the teachings of the Qur'an, are decent, faithful, and peaceful. We use the terms "Islamicism" and "radical Islamicist" to refer to the violent, extremist, and radically intolerant religious-political movement that now threatens the world, including the Muslim world.

This radical, violent movement opposes not only certain U.S. and western policies—some signatories to this letter also oppose some of those policies—but also a foundational principle of the modern world, religious tolerance, as well as those fundamental human rights, in particular freedom of conscience and religion, that are enshrined in the United Nations Universal Declaration of Human Rights, and that must be the basis of any civilization oriented to human flourishing, justice, and peace.

This extremist movement claims to speak for Islam, but betrays fundamental Islamic principles. Islam sets its face *against* moral atrocities. For example, reflecting the teaching of the Qur'an and the example of the Prophet [Mohammed], Muslim scholars through the centuries have taught that struggle in the path of God (i.e., *jihad*) forbids the deliberate killing of noncombatants, and requires that military action be undertaken only at the behest of legitimate public authorities. They remind us forcefully that Islam, no less than Christianity, Judaism, and other religions, is threatened and potentially degraded by these profaners who invoke God's name to kill indiscriminately.

Thwarting Aggression

We recognize that movements claiming the mantle of religion also have complex political, social, and demographic dimensions, to which due attention must be paid. At the same time, philosophy matters, and the animating philosophy of this radical Islamicist movement, in its contempt for human life, and by viewing the world as a life-and-death struggle between believers and unbelievers (whether non-radical Muslims, Jews, Christians, Hindus, or others), clearly denies the equal dignity of all persons and, in doing so, betrays religion and rejects the very foundation of civilized life and the possibility of peace among nations.

Most seriously of all, the mass murders of September 11 demonstrated, arguably for the first time, that this movement now possesses not only the openly stated desire, but also the capacity and expertise—including possible access to, and willingness to use, chemical, biological, and nuclear weapons—to wreak massive, horrific devastation on its intended targets.

Those who slaughtered more than 3,000 persons on September 11 and who, by their own admission, want nothing more than to do it again, constitute a clear and present danger to all people of goodwill everywhere in the world, not just the United States. Such acts are a pure example of naked aggression against innocent human life, a world-threatening evil that clearly requires the use of force to remove it.

Organized killers with global reach now threaten all of us. In the name of universal human morality, and fully conscious of the restrictions and requirements of a just war, we support our government's, and our society's, decision to use force of arms against them.

"To wage war may only seed the clouds for future acts of terror."

War Is the Wrong Response to Terrorism

Progressive

The United States should not respond to the September 11, 2001, terrorist attacks with war, the *Progressive* asserts in the following viewpoint. According to the magazine, war is an inappropriate response because it may lead to hate crimes against Arab-Americans and Muslim-Americans, could provoke further acts of terrorism, and may threaten Americans' civil liberties. The *Progressive* argues that rather than rely on a military response to terrorism, the U.S. government should instead reevaluate its foreign policy, which has angered people across the world and given rise to terrorists. *Progressive* is a left-wing magazine.

As you read, consider the following questions:
1. Why is the *Progressive* concerned about the comparison between the September 11, 2001, terrorist attacks and the attack on Pearl Harbor during World War II?
2. According to the magazine, which U.S. foreign policies have unintentionally aided the recruitment of terrorists?
3. In the *Progressive*'s view, what must the United States do in Colombia to prove it "abhors the killing of innocent people"?

"The Toll of Terror," *Progressive*, vol. 65, October 2001, pp. 8–11. Copyright © 2001 by The Progressive, Inc., 409 East Main Street, Madison, WI 53703. Reproduced by permission.

W e write just one day after the terrible terrorist attack [of September 11, 2001] on New York City and the Pentagon. We are in shock, as is the rest of the nation. We grieve for the thousands who died, the thousands who are wounded, and their families.

But we resist the call to arms, and we are made sick by the blood lust in the media and among the populace.

The United States should protect itself and its citizens— no doubt. That is a constitutional requirement, and the obligation of all nation states. But to wage war may only seed the clouds for future acts of terror. And to act precipitously, as it seems [President] George W. Bush will do, all but guarantees that the United States will hit some wrong targets and inflict needless suffering on hundreds—maybe thousands— of innocent people.

Recall the Clinton bombing of the Sudanese pharmaceutical plant in Khartoum in 1998, which destroyed much of the medical supplies for that country. Clinton said the plant was linked to nerve gas production, but never produced the evidence. Recall the missiles during that same bombing mission that strayed into Pakistan instead of hitting their targets in Afghanistan. Are we going to see more of those?

Bush seems indifferent to the "collateral damage" that any large military action will cause. But what kind of morality is it for Bush to decry the killing of civilians and then go out and kill some civilians himself?

A Backlash Against Muslims

Commentators tell us that this is the second Pearl Harbor. On December 8, 1941, [Franklin D. Roosevelt] got a declaration of war from Congress. No Congress has issued such a declaration since, though President after President has waged war. If Bush is to go to war, the least he could do is follow the requirements of Article 1, Section 8, of our Constitution. Otherwise, it will be another lawless act, and another diminution of our democracy.

The Pearl Harbor analogy has frightening connotations. Two months after Japan's surprise attack, the U.S. government rounded up Japanese Americans into internment camps. Now it seems highly improbable that Arab Americans or Muslim Americans will be rounded up, but what does seem quite possible is that the media's obsessive focus on a non-differentiated Islamic fundamentalism—mixed in with nativist sentiment that is always on the shell—will create a cocktail of hate crimes.

"We should drop nuclear weapons on all of Islam," said one anonymous caller, who left a message with American Muslims for Global Peace and Justice in Santa Clara, California.

"Islamic Americans in many cities have already been grappling with an angry backlash," *The Wall Street Journal* reported on September 12. "Salam School, an Islamic elementary school in Milwaukee, evacuated its 372 students after receiving two threatening phone calls. Meanwhile, Islamic schools in Southern California were evacuated, [and] a Fort Worth, Texas, mosque received a bomb threat."

The Council on American-Islamic Relations, based in Washington, D.C., recommended several security precautions be taken. "Those who wear Islamic attire should consider staying out of public areas for the immediate future," was one such precaution.

Do Not Give Up Civil Liberties

Meanwhile, the civil liberties of all Americans are under threat. ABC News conducted a poll on the evening of September 11 that showed 66 percent of Americans were in favor of curtailing civil liberties if it made them more secure. And officials were quick to go on the air with proposals that domestic surveillance be increased.

Civil liberties, like truth, are a casualty of war. It is not something we should roll over for.

In his primetime speech to the nation on September 11, President Bush said, "America was targeted for attack because we're the brightest beacon for freedom and opportunity in the world."

Not knowing with any certainty who the attackers were, it's hard to speculate on their motives. But many groups in the Third World have grievances that are more specific than the ones Bush mentioned, such as U.S. support for the corrupt Saudi regime, or Israel's ongoing occupation of Palestinian land and its suppression of the intifada.

No grievance, however, justifies the killing of innocent people. No grievance can make the acts of September 11, anything less than the ghoulish, heartless attack that they were. Those behind the acts should be apprehended and prosecuted to the full extent of the law.

America Has Cultivated Terrorism

But we do need to examine the roots of terrorism. And the United States has wittingly and unwittingly cultivated many of them.

In the case of Osama Bin Laden, Washington's chief suspect, it needs to be recalled that he was a creature of the CIA. In the 1980s, the United States put out an all-points-bulletin for Islamic fundamentalists to come to Afghanistan to fight the Soviet Union. Bin Laden was among them. "He is said to have received considerable money during the ten-year Afghan battle from the U.S. Central Intelligence Agency," the Associated Press reported on September 12.

(Ironically, many officials and former officials are saying the United States needs to loosen up the laws that restrict the CIA from recruiting people with unsavory human-rights records. These officials say we need to increase our "human assets," but what does that mean: We're going to put more Bin Ladens on the payroll?)

Ahmed Rashid's latest book, *Taliban* (Yale University Press, 2000), quotes Bin Laden as saying that American officers helped him set up his first camp in Afghanistan. "The weapons were supplied by the Americans, the money by the Saudis," he says in the book.

Rashid gives the background: "Between 1982 and 1992, some 35,000 Muslim radicals from forty-three Islamic countries in the Middle East, North and East Africa, Central Asia, and the Far East would pass their baptism under fire with the Afghan Mujaheddin. Tens of thousands more foreign Muslim radicals came to study, along the Afghan border. Eventually, more than 100,000 Muslim radicals were to have direct contact with Pakistan and Afghanistan and be influenced by the jihad.

"In camps near Peshawar and in Afghanistan, these radicals met each other for the first time and studied, trained, and fought together. It was the first opportunity for most of them to learn about Islamic movements in other countries, and they forged tactical and ideological links that would serve them well in the future. The camps became virtual universities for future Islamic radicalism.

"None of the intelligence agencies involved wanted to consider the consequences of bringing together thousands of Islamic radicals from all over the world. 'What was more important in the worldview of history? The Taliban or the fall of the Soviet Empire? A few stirred-up Muslims or the liberation of Central Europe and the end of the Cold War?' said Zbigniew Brzezinski, a former U.S. National Security Adviser."

A Dangerous "Blowback"

This boomerang effect is what intelligence officers call "blowback." And what is blowing back is a virulent strain of religious fundamentalism, and a large cadre of Muslim fanatics trained in modern warfare.

Bin Laden became further radicalized during the Gulf War [fought in 1991, the United States liberated Kuwait after that country had been occupied by Iraq]. He "openly accused Saudi Arabia's King Fahd of selling the holy sites of Islam to the United States," the [Associated Press] noted.

With that, he was off and running, first to the Sudan, and then back to Afghanistan.

Other U.S. policies have also served, unwittingly, as recruiting calls for terrorists. The sanctions against Iraq (and the regular bombings that have occurred in the years since the Gulf War) have appalled much of the world. And unconditional U.S. support for Israel, its chief ally in the Middle East, has enraged the Muslim world. Israel's thirty-four-year occupation of Palestinian land and its ongoing repression of Palestinians during the second intifada have raised tensions not only in the Middle East but throughout the Arab and Muslim world.

These may be some of the contributing factors behind the targeting of America. Others include: global poverty, bigotries of all stripes, nationalism, and a religious fanaticism that says any means—no matter how gruesome—are justified in the service of the cause.

War Is Not the Answer

To note these factors is not, by any means, to justify the actions of the terrorists. It is only to suggest that the United States should be careful not to pursue policies that are unjust or needlessly inflammatory. The United States will not be able to preempt the ravings of every madman, but it can see to it that it does not send thousands of people into the arms of such madmen.

The calls for retribution came swiftly, and from all quarters. One poll showed more than 90 percent of the American people in favor of military action. Another said two-thirds were in favor even if it meant that innocent lives would be lost.

But what will an attack achieve?

Bush appears to be planning a huge military action, perhaps including the bombing and invasion of Afghanistan. Other targets may be on the boards. How many innocent people will die in this act of vengeance against the killing of innocent people?

And how many seeds of terror will the U.S. retaliation sow?

We should remember that when President [Ronald] Reagan sent jets to bomb Muammar Qaddafi's tent in April 1986, a raid that killed one of Qaddafi's kids, it spurred its own act of revenge. A Libyan agent was convicted of the 1988 downing of Pan Am Flight 103 over Lockerbie, Scotland, which killed 270 people. Prosecutors said the agent was out to settle the score.

This cycle of violence must be broken. The time to break it is now.

Not Yet a "Good" Nation

One last point. George W. Bush said this is a conflict of "good versus evil." But the United States has a long way to go before it can put the halo of "good" over its head.

If the United States truly abhors the killing of innocent people, it must stop the killing of innocent people in Iraq with the weapon of economic sanctions.

If the United States truly abhors the killing of innocent people, it must throw its weight behind reaching a peace accord in Colombia [where a guerrilla war has raged for decades] rather than funding the military there, which is complicit in thousands of human rights abuses.

If the United States truly abhors the killing of innocent people, it must intercede with Israel and insist on the return of the Occupied Territories to the Palestinian Authority.

A little humble reckoning is in order, too. "The policies of militarism pursued by the United States have resulted in millions of deaths," the War Resisters League noted on September 11, 2001. And that is, indeed, the grisly record: three million in Indochina, one million in Indonesia and East Timor, tens of thousands in Latin America, thousands more in Africa and the Middle East.

"Let us seek an end of the militarism that has characterized this nation for decades," the staff and executive committee of the War Resisters League said on September 11, 2001. "Let us seek a world in which security is gained through disarmament, international cooperation, and social justice—not through escalation and retaliation."

Those are wise words, and we would do well to heed them in this time of terror.

The easy response is the military one. That's what the people clamor for. That's what the media clamor for. That's what U.S. precedent would require. But it is not the moral or the sensible line of action.

To pile innocent body upon innocent body will do no one—and no nation—any good.

"Realistically [the Road Map] is the best offer on the table at the present time."

Brokering a Peace Between Israel and Palestine Can Reduce Terrorism

Pat Lancaster

The international community has long sought an end to terrorism and violence in Israel and the Palestinian territories. The latest effort, proposed in 2002 by the United States, United Nations, Russia, and the European Union is the Road Map, a three-phase process that culminates in the creation of an independent Palestinian state and the end to violence in the region. In the following viewpoint Pat Lancaster claims that while it is not without flaws, the Road Map is an important first step to peace in the Middle East. Lancaster contends, however, that the map can only succeed if Israeli prime minister Ariel Sharon and his Palestinian counterpart Mahmoud Abbas can overcome criticism from political rivals. Lancaster is a writer for the journal *Middle East.*

As you read, consider the following questions:
1. According to Lancaster, of which necessities are the Palestinians deprived?
2. Why is Yassir Arafat angry with Mahmoud Abbas, as explained by the author?
3. Who is the "unknown quantity" in the implementation of the Road Map, in Lancaster's opinion?

For the first time in more than two and a half years there is a glimmer of hope for a Middle East peace process and the establishment of a Palestinian state by 2005, following the successful meeting in Aqaba, Jordan, between US President George [W.] Bush, Palestinian Prime Minister Mahmoud Abbas and his Israeli counterpart Ariel Sharon. However, there is still much difficult territory to be negotiated if the Road Map is to have any real chance of success.

The Palestinians and the Israelis have no reason to trust each other. And they don't. Neither side trusts President George W. Bush either. But both realise he is now probably the only person with a prayer of brokering a peace deal between them.

A Deteriorating Situation

Things have been bad before but over the past two and a half years of the Intifada [Palestinian uprising], the situation between Israelis and Palestinians [has] deteriorated to what must surely be close to rock bottom. The Israelis, enraged by the devastation Palestinian suicide bombers have wrought on the populations of their towns and cities, have enforced ever more vicious punishments and restrictions, including demolishing schools, hospitals and homes, frequently with the inhabitants still inside. The imposition of almost 24-hour-long curfews and the execution of a 'shoot to kill' policy that has claimed the lives of hundreds of innocent Palestinians as well as foreign observers—some of them in the Occupied Territories specifically to help avert the threat of physical danger to the Palestinians—have further exacerbated the situation.

The Palestinians are being herded into ever decreasing tracts of land and, in the case of the West Bank, suffering the humiliation and the dangers attached to being restrained there by an eight metre high perimeter wall the Israelis have constructed to cage them.

Israeli settlements have continued to mushroom in the hills above Palestinian towns and villages in direct contravention of United Nations rulings. The daily lives of Palestinian men, women and children have gradually descended into the sort of living hell most of us cannot begin to comprehend. Deprived not only of their liberty but also of water, fresh food supplies, the right to work, education—all of the things most of us take for granted—some have resorted to drastic action.

All life is precious and every Israeli death that has occurred as a result of fanatical suicide bombers is to be mourned. But it is the flagrant abuse of, and disregard for, Palestinian life that fuels the zealots of Arab extremist groups who demand reparation in blood. In the meantime, it is the ordinary citizens on both sides who have paid the highest price for the failure of their leaders to reach a workable solution.

Hope Among Arabs

Into this arena of murder and mayhem stepped the unlikely figure of President George W. Bush, the US leader who made clear right from the start of his term of office, he had no intention of becoming enmeshed in the Middle East imbroglio that had confounded so many of his predecessors in the White House. Yet it is this unlikely broker for peace who secured commitments from Israeli Prime Minister Ariel Sharon and his Palestinian counterpart Mahmoud Abbas to patch up their differences and begin working on a new peace deal.

At the June [2003] summit in Aqaba, Mr Sharon promised to begin confronting the settler movement he has nurtured for years and to work towards recognition of a Palestinian state. Meanwhile, Mr Abbas promised to bring the suicide bombers under control, call a halt to the violence and permit only law enforcement officers to carry guns.

To say there is optimism in Arab capitals would be to stretch a point. It seems we have all been here before. But alongside the feeling of deja vu there is also hope as Arab leaders watch with fascination from the sidelines. "Achieving these goals will require courage and moral vision from every side from every leader," President Bush announced. America is committed and I am committed in helping all the parties reach the hard and heroic decisions that will lead to peace."

In fact, George Bush badly needs to bring this deal off if he is to restore his standing in the Arab world. Many states, still reeling from the US invasions of Afghanistan [in fall 2001] and Iraq [in spring 2003] and unsettled by the State Department's vitriolic condemnation of Syria and Iran, eye the American leader with ill concealed contempt. Some suspect a secret US agenda that remains only partially fulfilled. On the Arab street the suspicion has turned to hatred. Iraqis and Afghans are shooting their "liberators" on the streets of Baghdad and Kabul. If George Bush could engineer a solution to the protracted, desperate plight of the Palestinians this would undoubtedly go a long way to restoring his severely tarnished honour among the Arabs.

The Demographics of Suicide Bombers

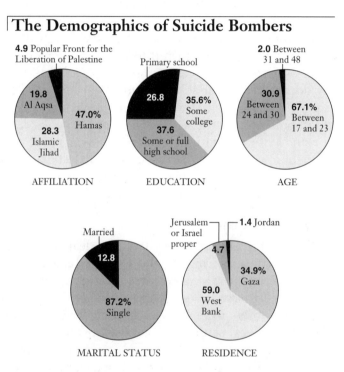

Christopher Dickey, *Newsweek*, April 15, 2002.

Ariel Sharon also needs this final accolade before he can willingly wind up his long and varied political career. His people crave a return to normality, an atmosphere in which they can go about their business without fear of suicide bombs and gunmen brandishing automatic weapons. Sharon would dearly love to be the leader who gives it to them. In order to make it happen the Israeli Prime Minister will need to make sacrifices but, it would appear, this has been fully taken onboard. "As all parties perform their obligations, we will seek to restore normal Palestinian life, improve the humanitarian situation, rebuild trust, and promote progress towards the President's vision. We will act in a manner that respects the dignity as well as the human rights of all people. We can also reassure our Palestinian partners that we understand the importance of territorial continuity in the West Bank, for a viable, Palestinian state," Ariel Sharon observed.

Mahmoud Abbas needs to see an end to the death and destruction that has torn his community apart. The Palestinians have sworn they will not be crushed, that they will continue the fight to the last man if need be. If the bloodshed continues future unborn generations of Palestinians are already doomed. The Palestinian Prime Minister spoke convincingly, "Our goal is clear, and we will implement it firmly and without compromise: A complete end to violence and terrorism . . . In order to succeed there must be a clear improvement in the lives of the Palestinians. Palestinians must live in dignity, be able to move, go to their jobs and schools, visit their families, and conduct a normal life".

An Imperfect Plan

Of course not everyone agrees that the deal brokered in Aqaba is worth advancing. In the Knesset [Israel's parliament], Ariel Sharon was jeered and heckled by right wing members of his own Likud Party for committing to the Road Map. Settlers were enraged by their leader's promise to dismantle illegal settlement outposts in the West Bank and former prime minister Binyamin Netanyahu is known to favour a rebellion in Likud's ranks to unseat Prime Minister Sharon. However, recent opinion polls show that an overwhelming proportion of Israelis are for the abolition of illegal settlements and the establishment of a Palestinian state, if it brings peace.

Palestinian Authority Chairman Yasser Arafat, who was excluded from the summit on the grounds that he had encouraged terrorism, was reported to be "furious" with his Prime Minister for returning from Aqaba "empty handed". Mr Arafat believes Mahmoud Abbas promised too much for too little return, a sentiment shared by groups such as Hamas, Islamic Jihad and the Al Aqsa Brigade, who launched a series of murderous attacks on Israeli troops to signal their displeasure. Many ordinary Palestinians also feel Abbas has promised things he cannot deliver. "He cannot control the Intifada, it is not in his power to do that, and to crack down on the militant groups could prove a very dangerous act", warned one Ramallah resident.

Certainly, the Road Map is far from perfect, particularly since it leaves two important points unresolved. It does not tackle the issues of sovereignty, of Jerusalem as an Arab as well as an Israeli capital, nor the "right of return" of Palestinians who fled their homes in 1948 and their descendants. These matters will be dealt with at a later date. However, realistically it is the best offer on the table at the present time, indeed it is the only offer.

If he has the will to carry his promises through, Ariel Sharon, with public opinion firmly behind him—if the opinion polls are to be believed—will weather the political fallout. The position of Mahmoud Abbas is less certain. Yasser Arafat still commands enormous respect. If he declares the Road Map untenable, its chances of success will be greatly reduced. The unknown quantity is, of course, President Bush. Tried and tested in making war, untried and untested in making peace, how he will help progress the Road Map towards the establishment of a Palestinian state by 2005 remains to be seen. As long as there is Israeli occupation there will be Arab resistance, many Palestinians feel they have little left to lose but their lives. The same is not true of the Israelis. Generous US aid has contributed to the majority enjoying a comparatively comfortable—even enviable—lifestyle. Before Ariel Sharon's fateful visit to the Al Aqsa Mosque in September 2000, which sparked the latest Intifada, the fruits of bilateral cooperation between the two powers had started to blossom. The Palestinian economy was on the up, with agriculture and tourism recording record levels. Israel was also a recipient of the fruits of peace. As its standing in the international community increased, so too did trade and tourism. War is an expensive business neither side can afford, particularly if President Bush decides to reduce the level of America's financial backing to Tel Aviv.

A Step Toward Peace

The Road Map provides no more than a glimmer of hope on which to build. Before Ariel's Sharon's fateful walk around the site of the Al Aqsa Mosque—an arrogant, conceited gesture intended to demonstrate Israeli sovereignty—there were already serious rifts in the uneasy peace that existed between Palestinians and Israelis. But at least there were no suicide bombers in Israeli buses, restaurants and shopping malls, or troops openly and systematically demolishing Palestinian homes, murdering innocents in their beds or allowing them to expire in ambulances at army checkpoints.

If the Road Map can help return us to where we stood before 28 September 2000, it may be possible to re-negotiate a better route the next time we reach the crossroads. Sometimes it seems that peace for the Middle East is still a million miles away but every journey must begin with a single step. Perhaps we should consider the Road Map, with all its faults, as that single step.

| *"The road map would create a privileged
sanctuary from which terror attacks could
be launched."*

Brokering a Peace Between
Israel and Palestine Will Not
Reduce Terrorism

Morton A. Kaplan

The Road Map, a step-by-step plan devised by the United
States, European Union, Russia, and the United Nations to
end terrorism and violence in the Middle East, is unlikely to
succeed, Morton A. Kaplan argues in the following viewpoint. He contends that the road map will fail because it
poses a significant security threat to Israel while demanding
relatively little of the Palestinians. Kaplan asserts that unless
the road map is reinterpreted and Palestinian prime minister
Abu Mazen is able to end suicide bombings and overcome
the interference of Palestine Liberation Organization head
Yassir Arafat, Israel is likely to suffer increased terrorist attacks. Kaplan is the editor and publisher of the *World and I.*

As you read, consider the following questions:
1. According to Kaplan, who created the modern state of
   Israel?
2. Why did Yassir Arafat start an intifada (uprising), in
   Kaplan's view?
3. In the author's opinion, why should European nations
   not be in charge of monitoring the road map?

Morton A. Kaplan, "The Israeli-Palestinian Quagmire," *The World and I*, vol. 18,
August 2003, p. 12. Copyright © 2003 by News World Communications, Inc.
Reproduced by permission.

There can be little doubt that the military campaign that overthrew [Iraqi leader] Saddam Hussein [in 2003] was brilliantly conceived and executed. However, an evaluation of the venture must rest not only on its military execution but also on how well its objectives will be accomplished.

Although the Bush administration believed, no doubt correctly despite the paucity of post-attack evidence, that the Saddam regime intended to produce weapons of mass destruction, that was the ostensible but not the determining objective behind the decision to attack. The determining objectives were undermining support for terrorism within the Middle East and removing the clash between the Israelis and the Palestinians as a focus for instability. . . .

History Has Been Misread

The hinge is the former Palestine. There is no doubt that virtually all Arabs believe that the United States has not been evenhanded in its treatment of Israel and the Palestinians. As Norman Berdichevsky makes clear in his commentary [in August 2003's *World and I*], that belief is a serious misreading of history.

Both Britain and the United States favored the Palestinians in 1948. The British even withdrew in a way that deliberately made the defense of a new Jewish state much more difficult against invading Arab armies. Israel nonetheless might have forced a peace that eventually might have produced a Palestinian state. However, the United Nations, backed by Britain and the United States, prevented this by forcing Israel to halt its military advances.

Contrary to contemporary myths, neither the United Nations nor the United States created Israel. The Labor Party under David Ben-Gurion and the Haganah[1] created Israel despite six invading armies and the machinations of the British army. No Palestinian state was created because no basis for it existed at that time.

What is virtually unknown today is that the respective British and American foreign and war departments were

1. an underground military organization that operated between 1920 and 1948, before Israel was officially declared a state

hotbeds of vicious anti-Semitism, inculcated at the Oxbridge complex [Oxford and Cambridge Universities] and the Ivy League, that had to be restrained by Winston Churchill and Harry Truman. Israel survived only because the Soviet Union permitted it to purchase weapons from Czechoslovakia with which it could defend itself from external attack.

A Sequential Process Will Not Work

The history of the case is one of missed opportunities as peace was sacrificed to other objectives. However, even now when peace is a central objective, the process is misguided. The United States made a major mistake in signing on to a road map based on sequential stages. It suffers from the fatal defects of all step-by-step proposals since 1974 to solve this problem.

Unequal Treatment

By omission as much as by commission, the United States and other democracies [in implementing a peace settlement known as the Road Map] have encouraged radical Palestinians and their supporters to cling to their dream of eliminating the Jewish state. They have acquiesced in and thereby promoted the separate and unequal treatment of Israel as a member state of the community of nations. They have truckled to, and pressured Israel to reach an accommodation with, the most radical elements among its adversaries, while subsidizing and turning a blind eye to the culture of violence in which generations of those adversaries have been raised. When it comes to the workings of anti-Semitism, they have chosen not to absorb, and not to act upon, the indelible lessons of history.

In late March [2003], President [George W.] Bush's national security adviser Condoleezza Rice remarked that although the administration welcomed "comments" on the roadmap, the document itself was not susceptible of "renegotiation." If true, that is a pity. A road map to peace is a fine thing, but if it is based in denial and wishful thinking it will be rightly doomed.

Abraham D. Sofaer, *Commentary*, May 2003.

There are interim measures that can be taken that likely would be helpful. A case can be made for freezing settlements and dismantling illegal settlements as a goodwill gesture to [Palestinian prime minister] Abu Mazen. But the steps that Israel can afford in the absence of a comprehensive settlement are limited. Abu Mazen might respond by exercising real control over terrorists in a limited area. But the steps that he can take are also limited in the absence of a comprehensive settlement.

The crucial problem is that the road map would create a privileged sanctuary from which terror attacks could be launched and within which missiles could be secured from nearby terrorist states. The Israelis see this as a not unlikely prospect because [Palestinian Authority leader Yassir] Arafat has never genuinely accepted a two-state solution.

He started an intifada that would include terrorism inside Israel to undermine its will to resist. He speaks, as he always has, out of both sides of his mouth. Even with respect to terror attacks by Hamas that he did not order, he only pretended to arrest terrorists. He let them out of jail within weeks while transmitting funds to the families of their suicide bombers.

Arafat continues to interfere with Abu Mazen, who has minimal support among the Palestinians. Even Abu Mazen's efforts to cajole Hamas to stop suicide attacks are likely to fail despite the fact that he has not even asked for a pledge to refrain from such tactics if and when the Palestinians gain their state. He knows the terrorists would reject it.

Reinterpretation Is Required

Thus, Israel is being asked to agree to a staged agreement in which it would be left with even less assurance than it has today. Only an agreement that genuinely met Israel's security concerns could possibly be acceptable. Such an agreement cannot be achieved unless the road map is reinterpreted.

That the steps of the existing road map could be monitored by the votes of the European signatories to the road map in a manner consistent with Israeli security is a nonstarter. Only President [George W.] Bush can be trusted. The Europeans lack credibility because they are more interested in getting rid of the problem in order to stimulate trade than in acting as honest brokers.

Although I doubt that Abu Mazen can find the strength to

agree to a settlement that Israel can afford to accept, the administration surely must try to achieve this. There are some positions that have not been discussed that might help to reach a mutually acceptable agreement. However, if this is to occur, the situation needs to be analyzed not in abstract formally equal terms but in terms of the asymmetrical conditions that affect the needs of both parties.

The concept of a Palestinian state by 2005 is a good one. A coalition government in Israel that can make goodwill gestures is desirable. Even a few legal settlements might be disbanded provided that the Palestinians gave something, even if only of a symbolic nature, in return. But the step-by-step procedure is a guarantee for failure, because there is no step-by-step agreement possible that will not impact asymmetrically upon the parties. Hence, there is no step-by-step agreement that the parties can mutually accept.

It is possible to discuss various aspects of a settlement in sequence, but only on the understanding that no major changes will be made in the crucial circumstances of the parties until a complete agreement is reached that is ratified by votes of the respective populations in the two territories and not merely by their representatives. If such an agreement does not have solid support, it cannot be made to work.

Periodical Bibliography

The following articles have been selected to supplement the diverse views presented in this chapter.

Anne Applebaum   "The *New* New World Order," *Hoover Digest*, Summer 2002.

Pino Arlacchi   "Coordinating International Cooperation," *UN Chronicle*, September/November 2001.

Richard Cohen   "Using Torture to Fight Terror," *Washington Post National Weekly Edition*, March 10–16, 2003.

Alan W. Dowd   "Civilization's Reluctant Warrior," *World & I*, January 2002.

Neve Gordon   "Sharon's Lessons in Terror," *In These Times*, April 15, 2002.

Tony Judt   "The Road to Nowhere," *New York Review of Books*, May 9, 2002.

Omar Ibrahim Karsou, Richard Perle, and Bernard Lewis   "Palestine's Emerging Democratic Alternative: A Symposium," *American Outlook*, Fall 2002.

Tony Klug   "Is There Life After the Road Map?" *Tikkun*, July/August 2003.

E.V. Kontorovich   "Make Them Talk," *Wall Street Journal*, June 18, 2002.

Jerome M. Marcus   "Terrorists and the Law of War," *Weekly Standard*, November 19, 2001.

David Moberg   "In Pursuit of Justice," *In These Times*, October 15, 2001.

Oliver North   "Bush Shouldn't Waste Time on U.N.," *Conservative Chronicle*, September 18, 2002.

Clarence Page   "Bush, Ashcroft Sell Our Courts Short," *Liberal Opinion Week*, December 10, 2001.

Karina Rollins   "No Compromises," *American Enterprise*, January/February 2003.

Abraham D. Sofaer   "The U.S. and Israel: The Road Ahead," *Commentary*, May 2003.

John M. Swomley   "Ethics of the War on Terrorism," *Human Quest*, September/October 2002.

For Further Discussion

Chapter 1

1. After reading the viewpoints in this chapter, do you believe terrorism presents a significant threat to global security? If so, which type of terrorism do you feel poses the greatest danger? If not, why do you think the threat of terrorism has been exaggerated? Explain your answers.

2. Scott Gottlieb contends that biological terrorism is particularly dangerous because deadly viruses are easy to engineer. Jim Walsh posits that biological terrorism is a rare occurrence that has been overhyped by the media. Whose argument do you find more persuasive and why?

3. In his viewpoint Noam Chomsky makes the controversial claim that the United States is a serious terrorist threat. He provides several examples of what he considers to be terrorist acts, including the bombing of a Sudanese factory—an act authorized by the Clinton administration. After reading his article, do you agree with Chomsky's views? In addition, do you believe a nation can be guilty of terrorism, or is that a crime that can only be committed by groups outside the purview of a government? Explain your answers.

Chapter 2

1. After reading the viewpoints in this chapter, what do you believe is the most common reason for terrorism? Do you think there are other explanations for terrorism that were not discussed in these viewpoints? If so, what are those causes? Explain your answers.

2. Ibn Warraq and Antony T. Sullivan both quote the Koran to support their arguments about the role Islam plays in causing terrorism. Whose citations do you find more convincing and why?

3. In its viewpoint, Hamas outlines why it commits violence against Israelis. Do you believe the organization's views (if not its acts) are justified? Why or why not?

Chapter 3

1. Several of the authors in this chapter evaluate the way in which America after September 11, 2001, became a nation of "us versus them"—"them" being people who emigrated from non-Western nations or whose appearance and religion marks them as potential threats to national security. Do you believe that the terrorist attacks have led to a divided nation? Why or why not?

If so, what steps do you believe must be taken in order to reunite the country? Explain your answer.

2. After reading the viewpoints by Michelle Malkin and Hank Kalet, do you believe the USA PATRIOT Act will cause permanent damage to American civil liberties? Why or why not?

3. Mark Krikorian directs a center that studies the effects of immigration while Daniel Smith researches America's defense policies. Given their respective backgrounds, which man do you think is better suited to determining the effects immigrants have on national security? Explain your answer.

Chapter 4

1. Alexa McDonough believes the United Nations is best suited to respond to terrorism because it can establish international courts in which suspected terrorists could be tried. Steve Bonta maintains that UN-created international agencies are more likely to destroy constitutional freedoms than end terrorism. Whose argument do you find more convincing and why?

2. In its viewpoint, the *Progressive* states that U.S. foreign policy has given rise to terrorism. The magazine details a number of instances in which American support of certain regimes has served as "recruiting calls" for terrorists. Do you believe that the *Progressive* blames the U.S. government for the events of September 11, 2001? Explain your answer.

3. After reading the viewpoints by Pat Lancaster and Morton A. Kaplan, what do you think are the strengths and weaknesses of the Road Map? Do you believe the Road Map will bring peace to Israel and the Palestinian territories?

Organizations to Contact

The editors have compiled the following list of organizations concerned with the issues debated in this book. The descriptions are derived from materials provided by the organizations. All have publications or information available for interested readers. The list was compiled on the date of publication of the present volume; the information provided here may change. Be aware that many organizations take several weeks or longer to respond to inquiries, so allow as much time as possible.

American Civil Liberties Union (ACLU)
125 Broad St., 18th Fl., New York, NY 10004-2400
(212) 549-2500
e-mail: aclu@aclu.org • website: www.aclu.org

The American Civil Liberties Union is a national organization that works to defend Americans' civil rights. The ACLU argues that measures to protect national security in the wake of terrorist attacks should not compromise civil liberties. Its publications include "Civil Liberties After 9-11: The ACLU Defends Freedom" and "National ID Cards: 5 Reasons Why They Should Be Rejected."

Anti-Defamation League (ADL)
823 United Nations Plaza, New York, NY 10017
(212) 885-7700 • fax: (212) 867-0779
website: www.adl.org

The Anti-Defamation League is a human relations organization that fights all forms of prejudice and bigotry. The website features extensive information on Israel, the Middle East, and terrorism, including information on terrorist groups and articles such as "Terrorism and Moral Clarity" and "Give Security Agencies More Room to Fight Terrorism." The ADL also publishes the bimonthly online newsletter, *Frontline*.

Brookings Institution
1775 Massachusetts Ave. NW, Washington, DC 20036
(202) 797-6000 • fax: (202) 797-6004
e-mail: brookinfo@brook.edu • website: www.brook.edu

The Brookings Institution conducts foreign policy research and analyzes global events and their impact on the United States. The institution publishes the *Brookings Review* quarterly, along with numerous papers and books on foreign policy. Publications related to terrorism include "Nasty, Brutish, and Long: America's War on Terrorism" and "Protecting the American Homeland: One Year On."

Center for Strategic and International Studies (CSIS)
1800 K St. NW, Washington, DC 20006
(202) 887-0200 • fax: (202) 775-3199
website: www.csis.org

CSIS is a public policy research institution that focuses on America's economic policy, national security, and foreign and domestic policy. The center analyzes global crises and suggests U.S. military policies. Its publications include the journal *Washington Quarterly* and the studies "Protecting Against the Spread of Nuclear, Biological, and Chemical Weapons" and "Cyberthreats, Information Warfare, and Critical Infrastructure Protection: Defending the U.S. Homeland."

Council on American-Islamic Relations (CAIR)
453 New Jersey Ave. SE, Washington, DC 20003
(202) 488-8787 • fax: (202) 488-0833
e-mail: cair@cair-net.org • website: www.cair-net.org

CAIR is a nonprofit organization that challenges stereotypes of Islam and Muslims and offers an Islamic perspective on public policy issues. Its publications include action alerts, news briefs, and the quarterly newsletter *Faith in Action*. The CAIR website features statements condemning both the September 11, 2001, terrorist attacks and subsequent discrimination against Muslims.

Council on Foreign Relations
58 E. 68th St., New York, NY 10021
(212) 434-9400 • fax: (212) 434-9800
e-mail: communications@cfr.org • website: www.cfr.org

The council researches the international aspects of American economic and political policies. Its journal *Foreign Affairs*, published five times a year, provides analysis on global conflicts. Publications relating to terrorism include the anthology *The War on Terror*, the report "Threats to Democracy: Prevention and Response," and various articles.

Global Exchange
2017 Mission St., #303, San Francisco, CA 94110
(415) 255-7296 • fax: (415) 255-7498
website: www.globalexchange.org

Global Exchange is a human rights organization that aims to expose economic and political injustice. It believes the best solution to such injustices is education, activism, and a noninterventionist U.S. foreign policy. Global Exchange opposes military retaliation in response to terrorist attacks. Books on terrorism are available for purchase on its website, and the organization also publishes a quarterly newsletter.

Heritage Foundation
214 Massachusetts Ave. NE, Washington, DC 20002-4999
(800) 544-4843 • (202) 546-4400 • fax: (202) 544-6979
e-mail: pubs@heritage.org • website: www.heritage.org
The Heritage Foundation is a public policy research institute that supports limited government and the free-market system. The foundation publishes the quarterly journal *Policy Review*, along with papers, books, and monographs that support U.S. noninterventionism. Heritage publications on the war on terrorism include *Vital Role of Alliances in the Global War on Terrorism* and *Presidential Authority in the War on Terrorism: Iraq and Beyond.*

International Policy Institute for Counter-Terrorism (ICT)
PO Box 167, Herzlia 46150, Israel
972-9-9527277 • fax: 972-9-9513073
e-mail: info@ict.org.il • website: www.ict.org.il
ICT is a research institute that develops public policy solutions to international terrorism. Its website is a comprehensive resource on terrorism and counterterrorism, including an extensive database on terrorist organizations. Numerous articles on terrorism are published on the website, including "The Continuing Al-Qaida Threat" and "The Changing Threat of International Terrorism."

Middle East Research and Information Project (MERIP)
1500 Massachusetts Ave. NW, Suite 119, Washington, DC 20005
(202) 223-3677 • fax: (202) 223-3604
e-mail: ctoensing@merip.org • website: www.merip.org
MERIP is a nonprofit organization that has no ties to any religious, political, or educational organization. The project believes that stereotypes and misconceptions have kept the United States and Europe from fully understanding the Middle East. MERIP aims to end this misunderstanding by addressing a wide range of political, cultural, and social issues and by publishing writings by authors from the Middle East. MERIP publishes the quarterly magazine *Middle East Report*, op-ed pieces, and *Middle East Report Online*, which includes web-only analysis and commentary.

U.S. Department of State Counterterrorism Office
Office of the Coordinator for Counterterrorism
Office of Public Affairs
Room 2509, U.S. Department of State, 2201 C Street NW,
Washington, DC 20520
(202) 647-4000
website: http://contact-us.state.gov

The U.S. Department of State is a federal agency that advises the
president on foreign policy matters. The Office of Counterterrorism publishes the annual report *Patterns of Global Terrorism*, a list
of the United States' most wanted terrorists, and numerous fact
sheets and press releases on the war on terrorism.

Washington Institute for Near East Policy
1828 L St. NW, Suite 1050, Washington, DC 20036
(202) 452-0650 • fax: (202) 223-5364
e-mail: info@washingtoninstitute.org
website: www.washingtoninstitute.org

The institute is an independent organization that researches and
analyzes Middle Eastern issues and U.S. policy in the region. Its
website features several publications on terrorism, including the
anthology *America and the Middle East—Expanding Threat, Broad-
ening Response* and several *PolicyWatches*, among them "Patterns of
Terrorism 2002."

Website

Terrorism Research Center
(877) 635-0816
www.terrorism.com

The goal of the Terrorism Research Center is to inform the public about terrorism and information warfare. The site features profiles of terrorist organizations, essays and analyses, and links to
other terrorism-related documents and resources.

Bibliography of Books

Yonah Alexander — *Palestinian Religious Terrorism: Hamas and Islamic Jihad.* Ardsley, NY: Transnational Publishers, 2002.

Mitchell Geoffrey Bard — *Myths and Facts: A Guide to the Arab-Israeli Conflict.* Chevy Chase, MD: American-Israeli Cooperative Enteprise, 2001.

Daniel Benjamin and Steven Simon — *The Age of Sacred Terror.* New York: Random House, 2002.

Peter L. Bergen — *Holy War, Inc.: Inside the Secret World of Osama bin Laden.* New York: Free Press, 2001.

Yossef Bodansky — *The High Cost of Peace: How Washington's Middle East Policy Left America Vulnerable to Terrorism.* Roseville, CA: Prima, 2002.

Steven Brill — *After: How America Confronted the September 12 Era.* New York: Simon & Schuster, 2003.

Caleb Carr — *The Lessons of Terror: A History of Warfare Against Civilians: Why It Has Always Failed and Why It Will Fail Again.* New York: Random House, 2002.

Colin Gilbert Chapman — *Whose Promised Land? The Continuing Crisis over Israel and Palestine.* Grand Rapids, MI: Baker, 2002.

Noam Chomsky — *Middle East Illusions: Including Peace in the Middle East? Reflections on Justice and Nationhood.* Lanham, MD: Rowman & Littlefield, 2003.

Noam Chomsky — *9-11.* New York: Seven Stories Press, 2001.

David Cole and James X. Dempsey — *Terrorism and the Constitution: Sacrificing Civil Liberties in the Name of National Security.* New York: New Press, 2002.

Cindy Combs — *Terrorism in the Twenty-First Century.* Upper Saddle River, NJ: Prentice-Hall, 2003.

Isaac Cronin, ed. — *Confronting Fear: A History of Terrorism.* New York: Thunder's Mouth Press, 2002.

Alan M. Dershowitz — *Why Terrorism Works: Understanding the Threat, Responding to the Challenge.* New Haven, CT: Yale University Press, 2002.

Jean Bethke Elshtain — *Just War Against Terror: The Burden of American Power in a Violent World.* New York: Basic Books, 2003.

Thomas L. Friedman   *Longitudes and Attitudes: Exploring the World After September 11.* New York: Farrar, Straus, and Giroux, 2002.

Bill Gertz   *Breakdown: How America's Intelligence Failures Led to September 11.* Washington, DC: Regnery, 2002.

Danny Goldberg, Victor Goldberg, and Robert Greenwald, eds.   *It's a Free Country: Personal Freedom in America After September 11.* New York: RDV Books, 2002.

Rohan Gunaratna   *Inside Al Qae'da: Global Network of Terror.* London: C. Hurst, 2002.

Christopher Hewitt   *Understanding Terrorism in America: From the Klan to al Qaeda.* New York: Routledge, 2003.

Lewis Lapham   *Theater of War.* New York: New Press, 2002.

Walter Laqueur   *No End to War: Terrorism in the Twenty-First Century.* New York: Continuum, 2003.

Michael A. Ledeen   *The War Against the Terror Masters: Why It Happened. Where We Are Now. How We'll Win.* New York: St. Martin's Press, 2002.

Barry S. Levy and Victor W. Sidel, eds.   *Terrorism and Public Health: A Balanced Approach to Strengthening Systems and Protecting People.* Oxford, UK: Oxford University Press, 2003.

Bernard Lewis   *The Crisis of Islam: Holy War and Unholy Terror.* New York: Modern Library, 2003.

Bernard Lewis   *What Went Wrong? Western Impact and Middle Eastern Response.* New York: Oxford University Press, 2001.

A.G. Noorani   *Islam and Jihad: Prejudice Versus Reality.* New York: Zed Books, 2002.

Meghan L. O'Sullivan   *Shrewd Sanctions: Statecraft and State Sponsors of Terrorism.* Washington, DC: Brookings Institution Press, 2003.

Kent Roach   *September 11: Consequences for Canada.* Montreal: McGill-Queen's University Press, 2003.

James Ron   *Frontiers and Ghettos: State Violence in Serbia and Israel.* Berkeley and Los Angeles: University of California Press, 2003.

Barry Rubin and Judith Colp Rubin, eds.   *Anti-American Terrorism and the Middle East: A Documentary Reader.* New York: Oxford University Press, 2002.

Avi Shlaim   *The Iron Wall: Israel and the Arab World.* New York: W.W. Norton, 2001.

Marilyn W. Thompson   *The Killer Strain: Anthrax and a Government Exposed.* New York: HarperCollins, 2003.

Paul L. Williams   *Al-Qaeda: Brotherhood of Terror.* Parsippany, NJ: Alpha, 2002.

Howard Zinn   *Terrorism and War.* New York: Seven Stories Press, 2002.

Stephen Zunes   *Tinderbox: U.S. Foreign Policy and the Roots of Terrorism.* Monroe, ME: Common Courage Press, 2003.

Index